JUSTIFICATION AND THE FUTURE OF THE ECUMENICAL MOVEMENT

The Joint Declaration on the Doctrine of Justification

Edited by William G. Rusch

George Lindbeck
Walter Cardinal Kasper
Henry Chadwick
R. William Franklin
Michael Root
Gabriel Fackre
Edward Idris Cassidy
Valerie A. Karras
Frank D. Macchia

LITURGICAL PRESS
Collegeville, Minnesota

www.litpress.org

A title of the Unitas Books series published by the Liturgical Press

Cover design by McCormick Creative

1   2   3   4   5   6   7   8

Library of Congress Cataloging-in-Publication Data

Justification and the future of the ecumenical movement : the Joint declaration
   on the doctrine of justification / edited by William G. Rusch ; George Lindbeck
   . . . [et al.].
         p. cm.—(Unitas books)
   Includes bibliographical references.
   ISBN 0-8146-2733-1 (alk. paper)
     1. Justification (Christian theology) 2. Joint declaration on the doctrine of
   justification. 3. Lutheran Church—Relations—Catholic Church. 4. Catholic
   Church—Relations—Lutheran Church. I. Rusch, William G. II. Lindbeck,
   George A. III. Series.

BT764.3.J87 2003
234'.7—dc21   2003047491

Unitas Books

On the eve of his crucifixion, Jesus prayed that his followers "All may be one" (John 17:21). Christians believe that this promise is fulfilled in the Church. The Church is Christ's Body and his Body cannot be divided. And yet, the Churches today live in contradiction to that promise. Churches which recognize in another Christian community an embodiment of the one Church of Jesus Christ still too often find that they cannot live in true communion with them. This contradiction between the Church's unity and its division has driven the ecumenical movement over the last century.

The pursuit of unity will require more than a few mutual adjustments among the Churches. Ecumenism must involve true conversion, a conversion both of hearts and minds, of the will and the intellect. We all must learn to think in new ways about the teachings and practices of the Church. Division has become deeply embedded in the everyday life and thought of the Churches. Thinking beyond division will require a new outlook.

Unitas Books seeks to serve the rethinking that is a necessary part of the ecumenical movement. Some books in the series will directly address important topics of ecumenical discussion; others will chart and analyze the ecumenical movement itself. All will be concerned with the Church's unity. Their authors will be ecumenical experts from a variety of Christian traditions, but the books will be written for a wider audience of interested clergy and laypeople. We hope they will be informative for the expert and the newcomer alike.

The unity we seek will be a gift of the Holy Spirit. The Spirit works through means, however, and one of the Spirit's means is careful theological reflection and articulate communication. We hope that this series may be used by the Spirit so that the unity won by Christ may be more fully visible "so that the world may believe" (John 17:21).

Norman A. Hjelm
Michael Root
William G. Rusch

iii

Contents

Contributors

Edward Idris Cassidy

From 1990 until 2001 Cardinal Cassidy served as the president of the Pontifical Council for Promoting Christian Unity of the Roman Catholic Church at the Vatican.

Henry Chadwick

Professor Chadwick has held the Regius chairs of Divinity both at the University of Cambridge and the University of Oxford. He has been a member of the Anglican Roman Catholic International Commission and the author of numerous books and articles on patristic and ecumenical themes.

Gabriel Fackre

Professor Fackre is an emeritus faculty member of Andover Newton Theological School. He was a member of the Lutheran-Reformed dialogue in the United States. He has written extensively in the areas of systematic and ecumenical theology.

R. William Franklin

Dr. Franklin is the Bishop's Scholar in Residence for the Episcopal Diocese of New York. He is also dean emeritus of the Berkeley Divinity School at Yale University.

Valerie A. Karras

Professor Karras is a member of the faculty of St. Louis University. She is a patristics scholar and a member of the Greek Archdiocese of America. Her writings include both patristic topics and ecumenical themes.

Walter Kasper

Since 2001 Cardinal Kasper has served as president of the Pontifical Council for Promoting Christian Unity at the Vatican. Formerly a professor of theology and diocesan bishop in Germany, he has written in the fields of systematic and ecumenical theology. Cardinal Kasper is a former member of the Commission on Faith and Order of the World Council of Churches.

George Lindbeck

Professor Lindbeck is an emeritus member of the faculty of the Divinity School of Yale University. A Lutheran layman, he was an observer at the Second Vatican Council, and a member of the American and International Lutheran-Roman Catholic dialogues. He is an author of works dealing with systematic theology and Lutheran-Roman Catholic relations.

Frank D. Macchia

Professor Macchia is a member of the faculty of Vanguard University. An ordained minister in the Assemblies of God, he is a past president of the Society for Pentecostal Studies. He has published in the areas of spirituality and pneumatology, especially in the context of Pietism and Pentecostalism.

Michael Root

Dr. Root is professor of systematic theology and dean at Lutheran Theological Southern Seminary, Columbia, South Carolina. A Lutheran layman, he has served as Research Professor and Director of the Institute of Ecumenical Research in Strasbourg, France. He is a member of the Lutheran-Roman Catholic dialogue in the United States. Root has written or translated several works dealing with ecumenical theology.

William G. Rusch

Dr. Rusch is the director of the Foundation for a Conference on Faith and Order in North America. He was formerly director of the Commission on Faith and Order of the National Council of the Churches of Christ in the U.S.A.

Introduction

On October 31, 1999, a historic date in the history of the Western Church, in the city of Augsburg, Germany, a historic site in the history of the same Church, officials of the Lutheran World Federation and the Roman Catholic Church signed two documents, an *Official Common Statement* with its *Annex* and the *Joint Declaration on the Doctrine of Justification*.[1] With the stroke of pens on these texts one of the most divisive issues in the life of the Church was resolved. The Lutheran Churches belonging to the Lutheran World Federation and the Roman Catholic Church were declaring publicly and in a binding manner that a consensus in basic truths of the doctrine of justification exists between Lutherans and Catholics. They were also stating that as a result of this consensus the teaching of the Lutheran Churches presented in the *Joint Declaration* does not fall under the condemnations of the Council of Trent, and that the condemnations in the Lutheran Confessions on justification do not apply to the teaching of the Roman Catholic Church as presented in the same declaration.

Clearly the events in Augsburg on that bright autumn morning were without parallel in the history of Lutherans and Roman Catholics since the Lutheran Reformation of the sixteenth century. In effect, Lutherans and Roman Catholics were able to say officially that the major issue between them five centuries ago, which caused the split of the Western Church, was resolvable in such a way that a basic consensus on this topic could be identified between the member Churches of the Lutheran Federation and the Roman Catholic Church. They were also able to declare that the remaining differences in the understanding of justification were not of a Church-dividing nature.

The received documents, which made this unprecedented step possible, were neither the result of a process of compromise, nor a repudiation of the teachings of the Lutheran and Catholic Churches. Rather, the relevant texts built on the results of Lutheran-Roman Catholic dialogue, carried on at national and international levels for more than thirty years. The documents were also indebted to the work of Lutheran, Reformed, and Catholic theologians in Germany on the condemnations expressed in the sixteenth century by all parties involved in the Reformation(s).

If the *Joint Declaration* and the *Official Common Statement* along with its *Annex* are received, made part of the faith and life of the Churches, by the Lutheran and Roman Catholic Churches around the world, not all the Church-dividing issues between them will be solved, but a new chapter of Lutheran-Roman Catholic relations should be possible. Lutherans and Roman Catholics should have greater assurance that they proclaim the same Gospel of Jesus Christ and are indeed sisters and brothers in Christ. They should be able to see some of the historical and divisive condemnations being placed in a new category of nonapplicability.

It is understandable both before and after the signing in Augsburg that these documents, and the significance they represent, have been subject to an ever-increasing body of secondary literature. This development in both its critical and positive dimensions is to be welcomed as part of the process of reception by the Churches.

One of the questions raised early on in this reflection was whether this basic consensus on justification between Lutherans and Roman Catholics could be extended to other Churches with which both Lutherans and Roman Catholics have been in dialogue, especially Anglicans and the Reformed. Such a step would be of major ecumenical importance.

Within four months of the Augsburg signing, the Yale University Divinity School and the Berkeley Divinity School at Yale, under the leadership of the then-deans Richard J. Wood and R. William Franklin, sponsored a theological conference on the theme: "Justification and the Future of the Ecumenical Movement." The director of the Lutheran Studies program at Yale, Paul Stuehrenberg, also played a key role. The goal of the conference was obviously to begin testing the wider import of the *Joint Declaration*.

All the essays in this volume, with the exception of chapter 1, have as their purpose to explore the larger implications of the *Joint Declaration*. The majority of the chapters are the presentations made at Yale in the late winter of 2000. Three of the chapters were written later than the Yale conference and are included in this collection to expand the range of the discussion and to add new insights.

In the first chapter Professor George Lindbeck traces the history of the involvement of the Yale Divinity School in the ecumenical movement. He demonstrates how this theological school with its history and commitments is a logical site for one of the first conferences to study the *Joint Declaration.*

Cardinal Walter Kasper (then Bishop Kasper) presented a paper on the implications of the *Joint Declaration* from the Roman Catholic perspective (chapter 2). The Kasper lecture was followed by a presentation by Professor Henry Chadwick on the Anglican Perspective (chapter 3). The fourth chapter is an American Episcopal reaction to the *Joint Declaration* prepared for this volume by Dr. R. William Franklin. Professor Michael Root then provides the Lutheran perspective (chapter 5), and Professor Gabriel Fackre gives us the Reformed perspective (chapter 6). With the exception of Franklin's article, these first five chapters represent the Yale Conference.

The next (and seventh) chapter is a presentation made by Cardinal Edward Idris Cassidy at Notre Dame University in April 2000. As one of the key figures in the production of the critical documents, Cassidy (president of the Pontifical Council for Promoting Christian Unity at the Vatican until 2001) offers background and an evaluation of the *Joint Declaration.*

The last two chapters in the volume, respectively by Professor Valerie A Karras and Professor Frank D. Macchia, offer perspectives on the *Joint Declaration* from the Orthodox and Pentecostal traditions. Both papers were delivered at the meeting of the North American Academy of Ecumenists in St. Louis in 2000 and were part of a program arranged by Dr. Darlis J. Swan, then president of the Academy.

The discussion of the *Joint Declaration* and its larger impact on Churches in the ecumenical movement should and will continue. The editors of *Unitas* books are grateful to the contributors to this volume and to the Liturgical Press for making available another resource for this ongoing conversation about one of the most notable ecumenical developments of the last century with great promise for this century.

William G. Rusch

October 31, 2002

The Third Anniversary of the Signing of the *Joint Declaration*

[1] The Lutheran World Federation and the Roman Catholic Church, *Joint Declaration on the Doctrine of Justification,* English-Language Edition (Grand Rapids, Mich.: Wm. B. Eerdmans Pub. Co., 2000) and the websites both of the Lutheran World Federation and the Vatican.

Chapter 1

The University and Ecumenism

George Lindbeck

A good many people have expressed puzzlement over why Yale Divinity School, a university institution wholly independent of any Church body, should be sponsoring a conference that seems to them more ecclesiastical than academic. Why should it use its all-too-limited resources of time, energy, and money to celebrate a Lutheran/Roman Catholic sectarian agreement? To be sure, it is advertised as an ecumenical rather than denominational event, but the ecumenism with which it is concerned is itself ecclesiastical, for it has to do with the official relations of organized Church bodies. That is enough to make it "sectarian" in the way in which Americans now often use the word. The official ecumenical movement includes only Christians and excludes non-Christians, is composed of only some Christian Churches to the omission of others, and it has as its official and controversial defining objective the visible and, indeed, institutionalized reunion of separated Christian bodies. Perhaps none of those who have expressed puzzlement over Yale's sponsorship of this conference have had this entire litany of problems in mind, but some of the organizers thought that their concerns should be addressed. That is why this opening presentation is on "The University and Ecumenism."

The answer it proposes is that this conference, instead of being an innovation, is a continuation of a Yale tradition that started a half-century ago of support for the organized ecumenical movement, that is, the movement aiming at the reunion of the Churches. After distinguishing this movement from other sorts of ecumenism, I shall speak of this university's past and possible future involvement, but not

1

without reference to what was and is happening elsewhere: Yale's role in relating scholarship and ecumenism is, as I see it, more representative than unique. In the absence of scholarly treatments of this topic, this presentation will depend unduly on oral history culled from my own memories, but I trust you will bear with me.

What I have in mind when I speak of ecclesiastical ecumenism is the original modern variety, that is, the organized ecumenical movement in both its multilateral and bilateral forms that is generally thought of as beginning at the Edinburgh International Missionary Conference in 1910. As we all know, some of the other modern meanings which the word ecumenism has since acquired, such as the ecological and the economic ones, are devoid of religious connotations, but there are also uses which are more difficult to keep distinct from our theme. We need to remember in particular that the so-called wider ecumenism is not simply an expansion of a core meaning but is generically different. It has to do with interreligious rather than intra-Christian relations and is not part of the Divinity School's mandate in this university; the study of non-Christian religions (as well as undergraduate and doctoral-level work in Christianity) is assigned to the Department of Religious Studies, and it is presumably there that interreligious rapprochement would receive scholarly attention (though so far little if any of this has happened, at least at Yale). At any rate, the ecumenism for the study of which the Divinity School has primary responsibility is not interreligious, but rather intra-Christian.

Of this intra-Christian ecumenism, there are again two varieties, the informal and the ecclesiastical or, more analytically expressed, the adjectival and the substantive. Informal or adjectival ecumenism is what is now most often meant by the word, and raises none of the problems with which we started. Yale Divinity School has been nondenominational or interdenominational and therefore adjectively ecumenical since the nineteenth century. The inclusion of Roman Catholics and, far too rarely, Eastern Orthodox in the pan-Protestant mix is only thirty-odd years old, but whatever its material significance, this is formally simply a continuation of nondenominationalism. Faculty and students from different communions gather in this place to study, worship, and cooperate with each other to whatever extent they desire, and while this may help bring the churches together, it also may do the opposite for reasons which this is not the time or place to discuss. In any case, Yale's highly visible adjectival ecumenism does not by itself imply support for Church unity, that is, for ecclesiastical ecumenism; it is support for ecclesiastical ecumenism that those puzzled by this conference are questioning.

The story I shall tell in answer to this questioning has four parts. The first part deals with "University theology under attack" and could start in the eighteen hundreds, but my personal memories only go back to the 1940s, and that is where I shall begin the tale. The second part is concerned with the middle decades of the last century, and could be entitled "The Ecumenical Movement Rides to the Rescue of University Theology" or, more soberly, "The Heyday of Ecclesiastical Ecumenism." The third and fourth parts, which I shall treat all too briefly, deal respectively with the last thirty-odd years,"The Aftermath of the Heyday," and with the possibilities of renewal, of which this conference is perhaps a harbinger, in the relation of university-level theology and the ecumenical movement.

I. University Theology under Attack

The attack on theology's presence in the university began, as I earlier hinted, with the eighteenth-century Enlightenment, but probably did not reach its peak at Yale, a relatively backward institution in this respect in comparison to Harvard, until the 1920s, but I shall speak chiefly from what I remember from the '40s and '50s when theology was already staging a bit of comeback in part because it was empowered by the ecumenical movement. Yet the urge to expel theology from these once-sacral academic precincts remained strong; the character of this animus needs analysis if we are to understand the role of ecumenism in countering it.

There was during those decades a member of the Yale Corporation, this university's supreme and sovereign governing body, who was the son of an Episcopal bishop and also a person of national distinction. He was reported to have said, whether apocryphally or genuinely I do not know, that a modern university such as Yale needed a Divinity School as much as it needed a hole in its head. My impression is that he thought of himself as having outgrown his childhood faith, but he was not antireligious; he thought that the Churches and their search for unity were on the whole more beneficial than detrimental to the national welfare and accepted an invitation which was offered him to address the National Council of Churches on the occasion of its inaugural meeting in Cleveland in 1950. A late winter snowstorm prevented him and President Truman, who was also to speak on that festive occasion, from leaving Washington, but his undelivered and unpublished speech is available from the State Department, or at least it was some years ago. It is, as I recall, a paean of praise to the role of the churches in nurturing the biblical literacy (not biblical faith) which for him was essential to what Robert Bellah in the next decade was to label the American civil religion. (For those who may still be wondering of whom I am speaking, it was Dean Acheson, often regarded by people of my generation as the greatest American secretary of state and, with the exception of President Roosevelt, the greatest American international statesmen of the last century.)

As I remember it, the Yale Divinity School community was neither surprised nor much troubled by this unfriendliness. We were familiar with otherwise admirable members of the university community, not a few of whom regularly attended Battell Chapel together with the president of Yale, who also believed that the study of religion at the university level was intellectually null and void. Religion was not amenable to the scientific method or to truly serious and rigorous scholarship. If they knew such divinity luminaries as Professors Robert Calhoun, or H. R. Niebuhr, or Roland Bainton, as some of them did, they might admire their historical or sociological or philosophical competence, but nevertheless regard their theological work as vacuous. Religion did not belong in the university except as an object of study by nontheological disciplines. Departments of religious studies might be acceptable (although it was not until the 1960s that one was established at Yale), but not theology as a Church-related enterprise seeking to understand the faith for the sake of communities of faith. Faith could not be understood in an intellectually reputable manner except philosophically, or sociologically, or, above all, psychologically as, for example, by William James or Sigmund Freud. These nontheological approaches were not viewed as hostile to religion, but as neutral or friendly (even Freud and Marx were sanitized by revisionists), but they were thought of as leaving no room for theology and, by implication, divinity schools in a modern university.

For those of us who were studying both with these cultured despisers of theology and with the likes of Calhoun and Niebuhr, to mention the two divinity professors who most influenced me, this case against theology was a genuinely perplexing exhibition of blind prejudice by otherwise intelligent, honest and, in some cases, personally religious scholars, but in retrospect and with the aid of a little—but not much—of the currently popular hermeneutics of suspicion, it is not difficult to devise a plausible (and I think persuasive) explanation of what was at work behind the scenes. It was institutionalized fear of sectarianism. The Divinity School could perhaps be tolerated as a relic of Yale's Puritan past in part because it had become nondenominational, an exhibit of pan-Protestant adjectival ecumenism, but ecclesiastical interlopers, even if they were Episcopalians, had to be excluded. (The evidence for this that I myself had a chance to observe was the treatment of an eminent scholar, Berkeley Divinity School's Professor Edward R. Hardy, in the days when Berkeley's joining with Yale Divinity School was unthinkable.) If one denomination entered, then others would demand equal time and the neutrality indispensable to intellectual life would dissolve in divisive squabbles. Perhaps even Jews or, more fearsome than that, Roman Catholics, would have to be hired to teach their religions. In brief, unlike other Western countries, the American animus against religion in higher education, at least at Yale in the midcentury, was more a function of this nation's religious pluralism than of anti-Christian ideologies. It was internecine religious warfare—or, more vulgarly expressed, squabbling—that was feared.

II. Ecumenism to the Rescue

Ecclesiastical unitive ecumenism entered like healing balm from Gilead into this situation of potential strife: it reassured secularists and believers alike that theological scholarship (as distinguished from religious studies) is not inherently disruptive, and thus strengthened the place of the divinity school within the university.

To be sure, there were also other nontheological factors that enhanced the attractiveness of ecumenism and thereby also the acceptability of university theology. Some anti-Catholics were favorably disposed toward ecumenism until the time Rome itself joined the movement in the early sixties. Up to that point they hoped to use what had been a predominantly Protestant movement to counter what they perceived as a dangerous rise in Catholic power. (Remember, those were the days when Roman Catholics were not only on the upswing economically, educationally, and politically, but when they were seen as a demographic threat: their birthrate was much higher than that of Protestants.)

An opposing though not necessarily more reputable pragmatic reason for thinking well of ecumenism was its supposed anti-Communist potential, and of this John Foster Dulles, secretary of state under Eisenhower, is the best known example. He was dubbed "Mr.

Presbyterian" because of his active participation in the ecumenical affairs of his own denomination, but Church leaders, not least his fellow Presbyterian, Eugene Blake, resisted what they regarded as his transparently political efforts to utilize the ecumenical movement as an instrument in the cold war. Such pragmatic ecumenism, however, was sometimes characterized by a very different political orientation. Professor D. C. Macintosh, for example, who retired from his professorship in systematic theology at Yale shortly before I began studying here, was a Canadian Baptist, liberal in theology and evangelical in piety, who was convinced that the true unity of the Church is wholly inward. Because it cannot be externally manifest, he had no general ecclesiological but only specific contextual reasons for favoring, as he did, a worldwide federation of Churches including the Roman Catholics and the Eastern Orthodox. He was a pacifist who had suffered personally for his opposition to World War I, and he supported ecumenism in the belief that the Churches could thus be better mobilized in nonviolent struggles against Fascist and Nazi tyrannies as well as against other forms of oppression.[1] Such pragmatic or nontheological ecumenical enthusiasms do not survive the situations which produced them, and they have in fact largely vanished in recent decades. Their passing is not to be regretted despite the consequent waning of ecumenical zeal.

More serious is the weakening of the theological motivations for ecumenism that I remember in the divinity schools of my youth. Those motivations may not have been deep, but they were widely effective. It was taken for granted that God wills some kind of visible unity for the Church, but it was also believed that the questions of what kind of union and of how it is to be achieved are best left for later when other obstacles have been cleared away and reunion becomes a foreseeable possibility. Meanwhile, the prevailing sympathy for ecumenism ensured that the divinity school would produce in the ordinary course of its work the persons, ideas, and scholarship the ecumenical movement needed. Both the motivations and the situation were favorable.

Without anyone planning it that way, the ecumenical movement was closely and heavily dependent on the theological faculties whose place in the university it unwittingly helped to rescue and enhance. One description that captures the mood of the period, as I remember it, dates from 1948, the year the World Council of Churches came into being, and had as its author Wilhelm Pauck, the professor of Church history at Union Theological Seminary in New York. Ecumenical theology that is "both churchly and free . . . finds its foremost expression today," he wrote, "not primarily in the enterprises of the ecumenical movement itself but in the modern American interdenominational (or interdenominationally minded) seminaries and divinity schools." Their work "is unique in Christendom . . . a very positive product . . . of that diversity of Christendom which is represented by American denominationalism. Thus, it has come about that many American theologians pursue their work with a constant concern for the life and thought of all the denominations and not merely for that of their own . . . and that they are open to the thought of the Christian thinkers of all lands to an extent characteristic of the theologians of no other country." (Then follows a bit of chauvinism, perhaps excusable in a naturalized citizen [Pauck was German in origin], but not as the general mood that it was.) "It is time that American theologians should fully appreciate this great privilege and that they should consciously assume the leadership in the further development of the ecumenical theology. Their own Church situation has given them the methods of ecumenical theological thinking—the situation of world Christianity demands of them that they be fully applied."[2]

At the time these words were written, Union and Yale (together with Chicago as a distant third) supplied more of those with the doctoral degree (Ph.D.) who staffed Protestant denominational seminaries than all other sources combined. Pauck's conviction that the ecumenical theology of which he was writing would shape the future of what were at that time the culturally dominant religious bodies in America seemed justified; it helped account for the support given the movement towards Church unity by Yale. Harvard as well as other universities could also be mentioned, but Yale was perhaps the most notable. The Divinity School, for example, was host to the Central Committee of the World Council of Churches, provided much of the institutional infrastructure for the production of the Revised Standard Version of the Bible, cheerfully granted senior professors time for ecumenical involvement even though the extensive writing they did on these occasions never got into their bibliographies, and permitted junior ones, such as Charles Forman and myself, to take off whole semesters (in my case, five consecutive ones) for the same purpose. The increasingly multidenominational character of the student body and faculty (including a growing Roman Catholic presence after the 1960s) was more a fruit than a cause of this ecumenical involvement, but it provides infrastructure for further advances such as the present conference. What we are now doing is in no sense a novelty, but merely a revival of a tradition that never disappeared although it has been relatively dormant in recent decades. The reasons for this dormancy are the topic of the third part of this story, the aftermath of the heyday.

III. The Aftermath of the Heyday

The heyday of ecumenical enthusiasm peaked with the Second Vatican Council and the consequent entrance of the Roman Catholic Church into the movement, but already by the seventies, public interest began declining and the aftermath of the heyday began. That aftermath is still with us; official ecumenism attracts little attention and less enthusiasm when, as in the *Joint Declaration*, it bridges what was once thought of as the greatest doctrinal divide between Rome and the Reformation.

My remarks on the aftermath will be brief because it is familiar: we are living in the midst of it. During this period, the ecumenical movement, university theology, and the mainline Churches (that is, the Churches involved in the ecumenical movement) have diverged from each other and, perhaps in part because of this, have weakened in and of themselves; neither the mainline Churches, nor the ecumenical movement, nor university theology are as flourishing as they were in the middle decades of what is now the last century.

The disappointment of wildly unrealistic hopes is in part responsible for the waning of ecumenical fervor, though it should be added that for this the official dialogues are not at fault. They have for the most part been responsibly sober. None of us Lutherans and Roman Catholics who worked together in forty years of dialogue expected the reunion of the Churches in our lifetime, and even the *Joint Declaration* is more than some of us dared hope would happen in the twentieth century. Yet popular interest in and enthusiasm for unitive ecumenism has evaporated as it has become more apparent that the breach between the Eastern and Western Churches and, even more, between Rome and the Reformation will not be healed in the foreseeable future and, by worldly calculations, perhaps never.

One accompaniment of postponed hopes for unity is that interests have shifted. The questions that most preoccupy the organized ecumenical movement, as represented especially though not exclusively by the World Council of Churches, no longer directly concern Church union but rather focus on collaboration in social action—on what have come to be summarized as JPIC ("Justice, Peace, and the Integrity of Creation") issues. This is a change that became dominant as early as the 1966 Geneva Conference on Church and Society. The search for relevance or contextualization manifest in various ways in black, feminist, political, and other forms of liberation theology have tended to marginalize the classical topics everywhere, but more so in the ecumenical movement than in the Churches or the academy.

One result of this is that complaints that the World Council in particular is losing touch with historic Christianity are multiplying—especially from the Eastern Orthodox. They point out, for example, that for the first time in the history of the World Council of Churches, the motto of the Seventh Assembly held in Canberra in 1991, "Come Holy Spirit—Renew the Whole Creation," had neither a christological nor a trinitarian dimension. It is not only Churches but much academic theology that has been estranged from the organized ecumenical movement by these developments. As one German survey of these problems puts it, "Systematicians from the '50s to the '70s saw themselves obligated to formulate the great dogmatic problems in contact with the ecumenical world . . . [but] this direct thematic connection no longer exists."[3]

The classical doctrinal themes, to be sure, continue to play a part in the multilateral dialogues conducted by Faith and Order and in the bilateral ones between denominations. But these dialogues are now peripheral to most of organized ecumenism. Moreover, although the classic themes remain important in much university-level theology, they are far less likely than in the midcentury to be considered in relation to ecumenism, to Church unity. One reason for this is that the major shapers of the theological mind no longer assume to the degree that they once did that the visible unity of the Churches, however that is interpreted, is a proper objective. We are no longer in the days when Barth, the Niebuhr brothers, a Harnackian liberal such as Pauck, and a low-Church Baptist such as D. C. Macintosh could all agree with each other—and with Roman Catholics after Vatican II—that the goal of ecumenism is unity, even despite differences on how to institutionalize it. Clearly it is the conjunction of a variety of relatively independent factors that have led to what has come to be called the "ecumenical winter." But instead of further analyzing the past, let us ask about the future.

IV. The Future of Ecumenism and the University

In the light of the last thirty years or so, as we have seen, Yale's staging of the present conference may seem strange—not because it is innovative, but because it is old-fashioned. It looks like a throwback to midcentury when the desirability of the visible or institutional unity of the church was axiomatic, and when doctrinal agreement was emphasized as a necessary even if not sufficient precondition for unity. It is true that there was then no *Joint Declaration* to celebrate, but if there had been, if the necessary dialogues had already taken place, a university conference similar to the one we are holding would have seemed completely normal. It also would have consisted of lectures by learned academics skilled in classic historical and systematic disciplines, not one of them representing any of the new developments of recent decades that we have just reviewed. It is almost as if this conference were taking place in a time warp, as if nothing had happened since the middle decades of what is now the last century.

To this way of thinking, those decades were themselves an anomalous interruption of the otherwise relatively continuous Enlightenment erosion of doctrine and Church structures over the last two hundred years. What, however, if the influence of the Enlightenment on modern and postmodern religious developments is itself coming to an end? What if it is the currently regnant theologies with their indifference to unitive ecumenism that are the anomaly? Perhaps, in our post-Constantinian yet increasingly globalist age, the visible unity of the Christian Churches, no doubt in post-Constantinian forms, will come to seem more and more important.

Every plausible futuristic scenario has its plausible alternatives, but it is well to meditate on only one at a time. Our task in this essay is to picture the present conference as a harbinger of the future and leave contrary possibilities for some other occasion. Let us imagine that the tectonic plates of our culture are shifting in such a way as to encourage Christians once again to return to their ecumenical roots. We can start with what for some cultural analysts (non-Christian ones, by the way) has become the fashionable "idea that religious identity now competes with race, sex and ethnicity as a central aspect of how Americans define themselves" (along with, needless to say, many others).[4] This is a sharp reversal of the secularizing and community-dissolving trends of the last several generations. The argument is that a religious communal identity becomes an increasingly attractive alternative to the loneliness, anomie, depression, and meaninglessness characteristic of purportedly autonomous and self-actualizing individuals inhabiting the globalizing consumerist society of twenty-first-century capitalism. In order to provide such an alternative, however, Churches can no longer chiefly rely on ordinary familial and communal processes of socialization to transmit and sustain identity. These processes may have sufficed in premodern societies or in historically Christian modernizing ones, but not in what is now fashionably called postmodernism. The primary need in our day is for doctrinally normed and community-oriented catechesis, life, and worship analogous, though not identical, to the practices that enabled churches to survive and grow amidst the religiously pluralistic and wholly non-Christian cultures of the first centuries. Identity-conferring particularistic (or, less accurately in our day, "local") communities of faith are the first condition for the resurgence of unitive ecumenism.

The second condition, needless to say, is the perceived need for unity. Perception of this need has declined, we have observed, in the historically mainline Churches that brought the ecumenical movement into being, but it is increasing among the Pentecostals and conservative Evangelicals who are much the fastest growing portions of the Christian family. They are more and more attempting to resolve or mitigate classic (and debilitating) doctrinal conflicts, not least the ones associated with this conference, although their suspicions of organized ecumenism remain strong. Yet those who take fellow Christians seriously on such issues as the doctrine of justification will in the long run find it difficult or impossible to evade the question of Church unity. To the degree that the practical possibilities of combining decentralization with globalization become apparent, Church unity becomes an urgent matter for all missionary-minded Christians (and among these the Pentecostals and Evangelicals are preeminent). Moreover, the decentralization of unity is already an ecumenical commonplace. How else can the Churches become, to cite the familiar formulation, a communion of communions truly united and yet genuinely diverse?

Universities, as we have seen from the example of Yale, can contribute to this quest, perhaps more now than in the past. Not that they are the only places where scholarly contributions can be made. Yves Congar, a friar of prodigious learning and reportedly the favorite theologian of Pope Paul VI, was the last century's greatest contributor to unitive scholarship, in the eyes of many non-Catholics as well as Roman Catholics, even though he was excluded from his country's universities. (These have been rigorously secular since the time of the French Revolution over two hundred years ago.) His achievements, however, could not now be duplicated. Le Saulchoir, the Dominican House of Studies that was long his intellectual home, no longer exists, the educational infrastructure that supported it has disappeared, and there neither has been nor now is any other country where a career as productive as his in isolation from major research centers is thinkable. Universities may not be indispensable, but they are helpful.

In this country, unlike France, there are research-level institutions, though only a handful, in which advanced theological studies are programmatically present. It is on their hospitality that the future, not only the past, of intellectually and communally responsible ecumenism in part depends. Among these institutions, Yale is perhaps uniquely well-fitted to exercise this hospitality both because of its longstanding experience and because of the extraordinary range of traditions represented in its student body and faculty. Those Protestant denominations that were the overwhelming majority when I arrived at the Divinity School in the 1940s are now a minority, and the faculty has widened to include not only Roman Catholics but also distinguished scholars with Pentecostal and conservative Evangelical connections (all this, be it noted, simply in the process of seeking the best scholars in their respective areas without regard for denominational affiliations). Not least, courses are taught and research conducted with exemplary understanding and respect for confessional variety. No place in the country is better endowed with what I called "adjectival" ecumenism at the beginning of this essay, and that makes the potential of the Yale Divinity School for "substantive" contributions so much the greater.

But does not sponsoring substantively ecumenical studies such as is represented by this conference constitute favoritism? Does not doing this for Christianity obligate the university also to provide for scholarship serving the communal needs (as distinct from the putatively neutral religious study) of, for example, Hinduism, Buddhism, Islam, and Judaism? The only principled answer is that such service is appropriate wherever the resources and the opportunity are available. As the proliferation of communally committed ethnic and feminist study programs demonstrates, universities have abandoned the Enlightenment myth that objectivity requires neutrality; they can no longer consistently exclude the intellectually responsible promotion of communalism on the ground that the communalism in question happens to be religious.

What is appropriate, however, is not necessarily obligatory, and the conclusion of this essay is not that Yale or any other university is duty-bound to establish the equivalent of divinity schools for all religions just because history and/or choice happen to have endowed it with one (or perhaps two, as in Germany). My argument is more modest: Yale Divinity School has a responsibility verging on obligation to promote, not only the adjectival ecumenism with which it is already well-endowed, but substantive varieties one type of which is illustrated by this conference. Judging by the past, Yale's future contributions to intellectually and communally responsible ecumenism could be considerable, and it would thereby benefit, not only theological studies, but universities as a whole, the worldwide Church, and society at large.

Notes

[1] Douglas Clyde Macintosh, "The True Church and Ecumenism," *Personal Religion* (New York: Charles Scribners' Sons, 1942) 232–77. See also, "The Baptists and Church Union," *The Crozier Quarterly* III (1926) 259–77.

[2] Wilhelm Pauck, "The Prospect of Ecumenical Theology Today," reprinted in *The Heritage of the Reformation* (London and New York: Oxford University Press, 1968) 361–73.

[3] Dietrich Ritschl, "Oekumenische Theologie," in Dietrich Ritschl and Werner Ustorf, *Oekumenische Theologie—Missionswissenschaft* (Stuttgart: W. Kohlhammer, 1994) 85:7–94.

[4] Jeffrey Rosen, "Is Nothing Secular?" *New York Times Magazine* (January 30, 2000) 45.

Chapter 2

The *Joint Declaration* on the Doctrine of *Justification*: A Roman Catholic Perspective

Walter Cardinal Kasper

The Ecumenical Impulse

Aside from all the terrible things that have happened during the twentieth century, the last century will go down in history as the century of ecumenical awakening. The ecumenical movement is one of its few bright points.

It started with the experience in mission lands that Christianity's credibility is called into question if Christians are at loggerheads with one another. The problem takes on even greater relevance in the religious situation of old Europe. Looking at Europe people have spoken of a drying-up of faith. Faced with such a crisis, we cannot afford to continue with old controversies.

Jesus' prayer on the evening before he died, "May they all be one . . . so that the world may believe" (John 17:21) is, so to speak, his last will and testament for each and every Christian as well as for the Church as a whole. Hence, division among Christians is disobedience and scandal. Only a reconciled Church can carry forward its rightful mission of reconciling.

How Far Have We Gotten?

With the Second Vatican Council, the Catholic Church officially declared its irreversible commitment to ecumenism. Since then she has entered into dialogue with all the Christian Churches and ecclesial communities of both East and West. In the dialogue with the Lutheran

Churches the doctrine of justification was prominent from the very start. It was over this that unity was ruptured in the sixteenth century. For Martin Luther this was the teaching by which the Church stands and falls. So it was not just a theoretical problem for Luther; it was an existential question about the core, the center, the heart of Christian existence.

After a difficult inner struggle, Luther discovered that we are not righteous before God on account of our good works. Rather, we are righteous because God accepts us as sinners. Justification is not a matter of our righteousness but of the righteousness that, unmerited by us, God bestows because of Christ's merits alone, as grace alone and on the basis of faith alone (*sola gratia, sola fide*).

The Council of Trent also condemned the Pelagian doctrine that a person can save herself or himself by good works. The question at issue, however, was not: justification by grace or by good works. Rather it was whether and to what extent God's action enables and stimulates the cooperation of the human person. The Council of Trent ended up by saying that we can cooperate in our justification, not by our own strength but animated and empowered by grace. The council also wanted to make clear that God does not merely declare us to be righteous but truly makes us righteous; that he makes us new within so that we are a new creation and can live as new human beings. Faith must become effective in love and loving deeds.

These doctrines have divided Lutherans and Roman Catholics for more than four hundred years, bringing great suffering to individuals and to many of the peoples of Europe. Nevertheless, in their common resistance to the inhumane unchristian system of the Nazis, in the concentration camps and trenches of the Second World War, many Catholics and evangelical Christians discovered that they were not as far apart as had seemed. United in opposing an inhuman and unchristian system they discovered that there was more uniting than dividing them. Ecumenical theology after 1945 was able to make use of these experiences. We could mention a whole host of theologians from both sides who prepared the way for what has now been achieved, particularly Karl Barth and Karl Rahner. We are like dwarfs on the shoulders of these giants. I could also mention Hans Küng, Harding Meyer, George Lindbeck, Wolfhart Pannenberg, and many others.

When the official dialogue was started after the council, it was already able to draw on the results of theological research. The very first document from the dialogue, the so-called "Malta Report" of 1972, laid out a wide-ranging consensus about the doctrine of justification.[1] The question was taken up once more by the dialogue in the United States, *Justification by Faith* (1985), again with the same results.[2] Even later, it was also treated when all the doctrinal condemnations of the sixteenth century were examined, after the first papal visit to Germany. The results are presented in the book *Lehrverurteilungen-Kirchentrennend?*[3] Finally, the last dialogue document that remains to be mentioned, *Church and Justification* (1994), concluded once again that there are no longer any Church-dividing differences over this issue.[4]

So the first thing we should note is that what is said in the *Joint Declaration* signed October 31, 1999, in Augsburg did not drop out of the skies; it was prepared by decades of specialized theological work and ecumenical dialogues. All the more surprising and painful, therefore, have been the reactions of some theologians. In this dialogue which has lasted for decades, there has been no question of easy shortcuts or of false eirenicism, or liberalism.

On the contrary, number 14, where the common understanding of justification is expressed, starts with the statement, "The Lutheran churches and the Roman Catholic Church have listened to the good news proclaimed in the Holy Scripture. This common listening together with the theological conversations of recent years, has led to a shared understanding of justification." We have studied the sources of our faith together and immersed ourselves in the Sacred Scriptures and our respective traditions. This gave us new insights which shed new light on the statements of the sixteenth century. Neither Church can give up the doctrinal statements of that time or disown its own tradition, but we were enabled to understand them afresh and in a deeper way.

So we neither discovered a new Gospel nor rejected what our forebears believed as expression of the revealed Gospel. We discovered again that this Gospel once and for all revealed is so deep and so rich that nobody, no council, and no theologian can ever exhaust it. It is by the gift of the Holy Spirit that we were able to deepen our understanding so that we could recognize and re-receive our respective traditions. This new perception and re-reception is a gift of the Holy Spirit. So the event of Augsburg was first of all not only the signing of a document but above all a celebration of joyful thanksgiving to God.

A second point is this: although the documents I have mentioned were produced by theologians and commissions which had been officially appointed, their results had no official status for the two Churches.

So, after these fundamental theological preparations, it was time for the Churches themselves to take up the question and deal with the results of the theological dialogue. Thus it was that the Lutheran World Federation and the Pontifical Council for Promoting Christian Unity decided to attempt a *Joint Declaration on the Doctrine of Justification*.

It is well known that this was not to be easy. What counts though is the result. The crucial thing is that through the *Joint Declaration* the Churches themselves, rather than just theologians or even groups of theologians, have reached a consensus or convergence. It is this that makes the *Joint Declaration* something new. On the Catholic side, it was approved by the Congregation for the Doctrine of the Faith and the Council for Promoting Christian Unity. Immediately after the signing, the Pope publicly expressed his approval and joy at what had taken place and has repeated his approval publicly on several occasions since.

In Augsburg the relation between Catholics and Lutherans reached a new quality and intensity. We held out our hands to each other as Churches, and we do not wish to let go ever again. Obviously this agreement is not directed against any other Church or Church community, or against the fellowship of the larger ecumenical movement. It is open to all, and is an invitation to the other Churches to join us.

Thirdly: The content of the *Joint Declaration* is stated in number 15: "In faith we together hold the conviction that justification is the work of the triune God. The Father sent his Son into the world to save sinners. The foundation and presupposition of justification is the incarnation, death, and resurrection of Christ. Justification thus means that Christ himself is our righteousness, in which we share through the Holy Spirit in accord with the will of the Father. Together we confess: By grace alone, in faith in Christ's saving work and not because of any merit on our part, we are accepted by God and receive the Holy Spirit, who renews our hearts while equipping and calling us to good works."

I think this is a very broad consensus, a consensus not only on justification but one which puts justification in the framework of the christological and trinitarian confessions of the undivided Church of the first centuries, a consensus on the center and focus of the Gospel.

In the light of this fundamental consensus, numbers 40 and 41 reach a twofold conclusion: (1) There is a consensus on fundamental questions concerning the doctrine of justification. Open questions also remain and these must be further discussed but they do not take away from the common ground that has been reached. (2) The mutual condemnations of the sixteenth century, in so far as they concern the doctrine of justification, no longer apply to the other partner today if this partner stands by what is agreed in the *Joint Declaration*.

So we are dealing with a differentiated consensus rather than total agreement. There exists full consensus about the key fundamental issues, in the exposition of the various starting points, yet different thought-forms and expressions, and different emphases and statements are possible. So the *Joint Declaration* does not repeal the Council of Trent. For Catholics it remains just as valid as it was before. But it can be interpreted according to our present understanding of the faith in such a way that Luther's doctrine, as set forth in the *Joint Declaration*, is no longer ruled out as opposed to it and thus Church-dividing. The differences that remain are not contradictory statements but ones that complement and complete each other.

In assessing the *Joint Declaration* it all depends where one stands regarding such a differentiated consensus. This idea goes back to Johann Adam Möhler, the best-known representative of the Catholic Tübingen School in the nineteenth century and one of the fathers and forerunners of today's ecumenical theology. In his early work, *Die Einheit in der Kirche*, Möhler distinguished between acceptable and even necessary internal oppositions (*Gegensätze*) which are mutually complementary, and heretical contradictions (*Widersprüche*) which are incompatible with the faith of the Church.[5] Complementary oppositions belong to life and are therefore signs of a living church which is on the way. To demand a full consensus would mean to make unity an eschatological affair. In this world only a differentiated consensus is possible, and this means that the one, holy, catholic, and apostolic Church is an organic whole composed of complementary opposites. Or let me put it like this: The Church is an image of the triune God who is oneness in diversity.

In the background lies a certain image of the unity of the Church for which we are striving: a unity which does not mean uniformity but a unity in diversity, or (as, above all, Lutheran theologians say today) a unity in reconciled diversity. The *Common Statement* attached to the *Joint Declaration* expressly takes up this model and has thus given it official confirmation by the Church. This is a no less remarkable result of the *Joint Declaration*.

Future Tasks and Challenges

The Pope has described the *Joint Declaration* as a "milestone." The image fits the situation exactly. We have reached an important staging post but are not yet at the final goal. The *Joint Declaration* is important even though it has limits. Its greatness lies in the fact that we can now give joint witness to what is at the heart of our faith, and with this common witness we enter together a new century and a new millennium. Our ever more secularized world needs such a common witness. Its greatness is also that it does not disguise its limits but openly names the issues that remain between us.

So, clearly, the signing does not mean everything has been done. Rather we have to ask how do we go forward now that the signing is over? We have to distinguish between the tasks on the ground, at the level of parish or diocese, and those from the point of view of the universal Church. The ecumenical movement is a multilayered process and on the Catholic side, it would be completely wrong to wait on Rome for everything. The task of reception takes place above all at the local church level. Nevertheless, I shall limit myself here to the level of the universal Church, and in particular to what the Council for Christian Unity can do.

First of all, we shall have to review the questions about the doctrine of justification that have been left open after the declaration. I am thinking, for example, of the particular contents of certain doctrinal questions, such as clarifying further the issue of "*simul iustus et peccator*" or the criteriological significance of the doctrine of justification. I am thinking in addition of further biblical work which the Roman response has called for from the outset. The Bible, for both our Church communities, is the document of our faith, and I have the impression that we can make further fundamental progress by more fully involving Scripture study in dogmatic questions. There might be a symposium of distinguished Old and New Testament scholars, for example.

Secondly, I ought to mention briefly the important questions still at issue between us beyond the doctrine of justification. From the Catholic point of view, there is above all the ecclesiological question. This comes to a head in the issue of Church ministry, i.e., the priesthood of the ordained, the office of bishops in the apostolic succession, and the Petrine ministry. The joint dialogue commission between the Lutheran World Federation and the Catholic Church has begun working on these questions.

A third and final point. Many Christians today no longer understand the formulations of the sixteenth century. That is especially true of us Catholics. Speaking about justification is not part of our normal catechetical language. We prefer to speak about salvation, grace, new life, forgiveness, and reconciliation. The real reason why we no longer understand the term, however, lies at a deeper level. We have all become too deistic, that is to say it seems to us that God has quite withdrawn from our world and everyday existence. So the question about the merciful God, which moved Luther so deeply, leaves us somewhat cold. We have thus to translate both the questions and the answers of the past into the language of today, so that they will stir us as much today as they would have in the past. We have to set forth together the heart of the Good News in the language of today so that it is credible and convincing.

This is not only a matter of translating a few dogmatic statements, and even less of lapsing into trendy jargon. We must delve more deeply and ask: What does God mean? What does Jesus Christ mean for us today? Is he truly the Son of God who redeemed us by his Cross and Resurrection? What does it mean, then, to believe in a merciful God? What does this imply for our life?

About all of this, the doctrine of justification wants to say to us that we neither can nor should "make" our own life or its fulfillment: that we cannot accomplish this by our own efforts. Our value as persons does not depend on our good or bad achievements. Before anything we ourselves do we have been accepted and affirmed. Our life is ruled by a merciful God who through everything and despite everything holds us in his hands. We are able to live by God's mercy. So we should be gracious and merciful towards our fellow men and women. For that reason we can bring hope to a world which is still disorientated and lacks a sense of purpose, indeed has become nihilistic.

Courage in Ecumenism

One more reflection to conclude. Many think that the process of ecumenical rapprochement is going too slowly. They even say we are making no headway in ecumenism. It is certainly laborious, and needs patience and a great deal of staying power. The *Joint Declaration* has shown that even today progress is possible. This can give us a new ecumenical confidence and momentum.

This is necessary even at this moment of Church history. I have the impression that we stand today at the beginning of a new stage of the ecumenical movement. When we look back we may be disappointed that we have not achieved Church unity. Therefore some speak of a crisis in the ecumenical movement. But we should be far more grateful for what we have already achieved. At the beginning of the century, which has now ended, nobody would have expected where we are now. It was a successful journey from isolation, hostility, and competition to tolerance, respect, mutual cooperation, and even friendship. We discovered our already existing real and deep though not yet full communion in Jesus Christ. The *Joint Declaration* has enlarged and deepened this already existing communion.

The next step to achieving full communion will not be easy. To be honest, there are not only complementary oppositions, there are also contradictions to overcome. And unfortunately there is the danger that with the sociological change we face today new contradictions in ethical questions may arise. Or perhaps it would be better not to speak about new contradictions but new challenges. In any case, full communion cannot be achieved by convergence alone but by conversion, which implies repentance, forgiveness, and renewal of the heart. Such conversion is a gift of grace too—*sola gratia, sola fide.* So in the end it is not we who create unity. The unity of the Church is the gift of God's Spirit which has been solemnly promised to us. Therefore theological ecumenism must be linked to spiritual ecumenism, which is the heart of ecumenism.

One day the gift of unity will take us by surprise just like an event we witnessed on a day just over some thirteen years ago. If you had asked passers-by in West Berlin on the morning of November 9, 1989, "How long do you think the wall will remain standing?" the majority would have surely replied, "We would be happy if our grandchildren would be able to pass through the Brandenburg Gate someday." The evening of that memorable day the world saw something totally unexpected in Berlin.

It is my firm conviction that one day too we will rub our eyes in amazement that God's Spirit has broken through the seemingly insurmountable walls that divide us and given us new ways through to each other and a new communion. Hopefully we shall not have to wait another four hundred years.

Notes

[1] Harding Meyer and Lukas Vischer, eds., *Growth in Agreement* (New York/Ramsey: Paulist Press and Geneva: World Council of Churches, 1984) 168–89.

[2] H. George Anderson, T. Austin Murphy, and Joseph A. Burgess, eds., *Justification: Lutherans and Catholics in Dialogue VII* (Minneapolis: Augsburg Publishing House, 1985).

[3] Karl Lehmann and Wolfhart Pannenberg, eds., *The Condemnations of the Reformation Era: Do They Still Divide?* trans. M. Kohl (Minneapolis: Fortress Press, 1980).

[4] *Church and Justification* (Geneva: Lutheran World Federation, 1994).

[5] Johann Adam Möhler, *Die Einheit in der Kirche*, 1825, ed. J. R. Geiselmann (Cologne and Darmstadt: J. Hegner Verlag, 1957).

Chapter 3

An Anglican Reaction:
Across the Reformation Divide

Henry Chadwick

Reaching agreement requires a sharing of axioms. Yet psychologically it becomes especially hard when the parties stand very close to one another and there remains a 2 percent which continues to cause abrasions.

The consensus in the *Joint Declaration on the Doctrine of Justification* is not only a remarkable millennial achievement by both parties to the discussions over several years. It is also for Lutherans a fulfilling of the aspiration for reconciliation which pervades the Augsburg Confession and much of Melanchthon's "Apologia" for it. At least I take it that Wilhelm Mauer's interpretation of the Augustana still holds the field, namely that, although some articles such as 28 have a militant tone, the Augustana's original intention was not at all to maximize differences, and where differences obviously exist, to wish to see them as being less than matters touching the foundation of the Church of God thereby prejudicing possibility of true salvation. A similar judgment is found in Hubert Jedin, great historian of the Council of Trent. Not that justification is a secondary or marginal matter. The issue is capable of the most direct statement: How can I with soiled hands and a mind assaulted by at least seven deadly sins, be cleansed by my Maker and made fit for the company of his saints? Medieval religion had human feelings of guilt near its center, relieved by the confessional and especially by the wise doctrine that during the waiting state after death the soul may be purified to be fit for a presence of God and his saints, the principle being reinforced by 1 Corinthians 3. It is not natural for us to imagine that we shall be ready for that at the end of this turbulent life.

"Finish then thy new creation; pure and spotless let us be," wrote Charles Wesley in his famous hymn "Love divine."

I am priest in communion with the see of Canterbury who would dearly like to see the day when Rome, Constantinople, and Canterbury can do more than have their picture taken at a prayer for reunion, though I am grateful for the symbolism of that; and, please God, let them be joined in prayer by a representative of Wittenberg. I suppose an Anglican is likely to speak of justification in a context of prayer and worship. Let me quote an Anglican country priest of the early seventeenth century, George Herbert.

Love bade me welcome: yet my soul drew back
    Guiltie of dust and sinne.
But quick-ey'd Love, observing me grow slack
    From my first entrance in,
Drew nearer to me, sweetly questioning,
    If I lack'd anything.

A quest, I answered, worthy to be here:
    Love said, You shall be he,
I the unkinde, ungratefull? Ah deare,
    I cannot look on thee.
Love took my hand, and smiling did reply,
    Who made the eyes but I?
Truth Lord, but I have marr'ed them: let my shame
    Go where it doth deserve.
And know you not, sayes Love, who bore the blame?
    My deare, then I will serve.
You must sit down, sayes Love, and taste my meat:
    So I did sit and eat.

It is a great honor to be here in Yale, not merely as an honorary son of Eli, but because in this Episcopalian seminary the dean is 100 percent alert to the necessity and urgency of conversations between divided Christians, and the university theologians have long included highly distinguished scholars. The ecumenical task is never easy. Firmus, fifth-century bishop of Cappadocian Caesarea in the decade following the schism between Alexandria and Antioch at the First Council of Ephesus (431), longed for a healing to come; yet he wrote that, once Christians have suspended communion, reconciliation seems all too much a striving like that of Sisyphus in hades in Homer's

Odyssey, forever condemned to pushing a heavy boulder up a steep hill, only to lose control of it every time he almost got it at the top. The shameless boulder tumbled down the hill, and he had to start at the bottom once more.

A contemporary of George Herbert, Joseph Mede, whose writings were deeply influential on Isaac Newton, once remarked that there are Christians who can pronounce anathema on their own doctrines if they are formulated in terms with which they are unfamiliar.[1] We all feel at home with our traditional ways of expressing things. That becomes problematic when the old ways of putting it originated in a polemical context, and therefore to believers on the other side of the battered old fence the words inevitably come to sound like a hostile snarl.

Roman Catholics, Lutherans, and Anglicans obviously share a whole tradition of spirituality and theology stamped with the legacy of Saint Augustine, even including the *Filioque* in the affirmation of the Son present with the Father in the proceeding of the Holy Spirit; Luther had it in the Schwabach Articles of 1529. Without the *Filioque* Augustine and most Western theologians after him feared that the Arians could drive a coach and six horses through the doctrine of the Trinity. Members of our respective religious communities have found on retreats together that in prayer and spirituality they have total mutual understanding. But past history continues to haunt us. Between Canterbury and Wittenberg progress in mutual understanding here in America has been heartwarming. Yet there could still be a problem about the givenness of the ordained ministry, already traditional for Ignatius of Antioch. Is the ministerial order made secondary, or less than God-given, by the doctrine of justification?

An apparently marginal example is treating deacons as being in holy orders. And perhaps there are good reasons for that. The diaconate is not mentioned in the Augustana, and that is surprising seeing that Luther expected the church in Wittenberg to need deacons engaged in works of charity, not merely "epistolers and gospellers."[2] One cannot have a deacon in holy orders without a bishop to ordain this person (one recalls that in the *Apostolic Tradition* ascribed to Hippolytus the bishop alone ordains a deacon and the presbyters are commanded to stand there quietly and to do nothing). And while Lutherans have strong convictions about ministerial succession, in that a pastor can receive laying on of hands and prayer only from pastors who have previously received the same commission, it is also true that where primary stress is laid on the functions of clergy as constituting their special role in the Church, it is not easy to think of deacons as in holy orders without being clear about their sacred functions. A bishop at the Council of Trent begged the council to be constructive and clear about the function of deacons. His question did not get answered. The essential point is that of keeping the traditional ministry as the sign and instrument of visible continuity. But of course Luther was right that the function of poor relief was important and that in the ancient Church a deacon did more than read the gospel and minister the chalice.

Both Lutherans and Anglicans feel close to Rome in fundamental theology, but reserved toward universal jurisdiction and the consequent centralization of control. Admittedly, practical centralization is a modern phenomenon in the history of the papacy. But on at least a dozen occasions the Council of Trent reminds bishops that they possess authority only as delegates of the Roman Bishop. We do not want everything to be either forbidden or compulsory. But in medieval times, to the Orthodox Churches in the East, it felt like a bone in their throat that while they certainly desired communion with the Latin West, the Western negotiators saw communion with Rome as inseparable from submission to papal authority and jurisdiction and the adoption of Western customs. A similar problem faces the archbishop of Canterbury who manifestly desires communion with Rome but would face a riot if not allowed to regard women priests as valid. What degree of diversity is compatible with authentic communion?

How painful this was can be illustrated by a comic anecdote from ninth-century Church history. In the year 869 a new emperor Basil I much regretted a recent standoff between the Patriarch Photius and Pope Nicolas I who had excommunicated Photius essentially, if not formally, on the issue of Roman jurisdiction over the infant Bulgarian Churches. Basil removed Photius from the patriarchate and reinstated his predecessor Ignatius. The previous emperor Michael III had written scandalously offensive letters to Nicolas, and though Photius never abandoned courtesy, he was convinced that Rome and the Franks had led the Western Churches astray in the *Filioque*, in requiring celibacy of inferior clergy, presbyters and deacons, and in refusing to recognize the Second Council of Nicaea in 787 as having ecumenical status. Photius at least had no problems about leavened or unleavened bread for the Eucharist, which became central to the negotiation two hundred years later. By that time East and West were arguing whether clergy properly should be bearded or clean-shaven. Joachim of Fiore suggested that this was prefigured in Scripture by Esau and Jacob.

Nicloas's successor Hadrian II mistakenly imagined that with Basil's pro-Western policy, the Patriarch Ignatius would concede Roman jurisdiction over the churches of Bulgaria. Notwithstanding this emperor of the East, Rome could happily see the Franks, no friends to his Empire, in effective control of a bellicose tribe in his backyard. Feeling in a strong position Hadrian sent legates to a council at Constantinople. The legates demanded that Greek metropolitans desiring communion with Saint Peter's see must sign a paper submitting in obedience to Roman authority. The Greek bishops signed but unhappily. A raiding party stole the signed papers from the legates' lodging, and the reasonably furious legates demanded action by the emperor, who got the papers back from them. However, the matter was not over; after the council the legates took ship across the Adriatic from Durazzo. The emperor arranged for the sailors of the Byzantine navy to masquerade as pirates and to recover both the signed papers and the legate's copy of the Acts of the council.

How central the question of justification has been in the mind and heart of Lutherans goes back to Martin Luther himself, for whom this was the indispensable criterion for evaluating everything else taught and proclaimed not only in Word and sacrament but also in ecclesial structures which seemed almost secondary. If you think episcopal succession no negligible matter, does that mean you have failed to understand justification? We may remember that the Council of Trent insists that one is free to believe some sacraments more important than others.[3]

Sixteenth-century English Reformers borrowed from the Augsburg and especially the Württemberg Confessions some language about justification in the Thirty-Nine Articles. These were approved in 1571 after Queen Elizabeth had been excommunicated by Pius V. It was a sequence of events like that in the general Synod in London (1992), where the narrow vote in favor of women priests went through after and perhaps partly in consequence of the Vatican's fairly negative reaction to the first Anglican Roman Catholic International Commission's report—a reaction which Cardinal Ratzinger has assured us was not intended to be so very negative, but the verdict was hard to read otherwise. It was certainly more negative than was hoped for by Cardinal Willebrands, who is to be mentioned with awe, high reverence, and personal affection.

The initial breach between England and Rome came with Henry VIII who was no kind of Protestant, and kept the Latin Mass to the end of his life. Bishop John Fisher of Rochester preached at the lying in state of his father Henry VII who on the day of his departing "heard a mass of the glorious virgin the Mother of Christ to whom in this life he had a singular and special devotion."[4] But thirty-five years later the son denied papal jurisdiction in his realm. Under Elizabeth, his daughter, that still remained the rub.

Henry and his brilliant if Machiavellian daughter (both Pope and Archbishop Matthew Parker of Canterbury concurred about her Machiavellian ways) both wanted a national Church, not to be governed by an Italian prelate. The attitude antedated the sixteenth century. Medieval conflicts concerning investiture, power to nominate bishops and abbots, authority to levy Peter's pence as a tax on the faithful everywhere at least in the West, left a legacy of tension. The Council of Basel in the 1520s had heard similar language. The bishops at Basel had resented the Roman curia, and then discovered that they themselves needed something like it if their own program was to be put into effect. Their program was "Reform of the Church in head and members." But both at Basel and at Trent hard words were used about corruption in the Roman Curia.[5]

In Europe of the fifteenth and sixteenth centuries every thoughtful Christian wanted reform. Peasants were superstitious, clergy seemed too money-grubbing, and in England people spoke of "pickpurse purgatory." The reform canons of Trent attack bishops using Church funds to enrich relatives, and speak of serious abuses even by cardinals and cathedral dignitaries. Pope Clement VII in 1534 had provided his nephew with the revenues of all vacant benefices for six months. A bishop of Venice who had never received episcopal ordination drew the income of his see; in Elizabeth's England a very protestant dean of Durham, William Whittingham, never received priestly orders, but he was a hero of war against France which may have excused him.

When the Council of Constance met early in the fifteenth century to end the great papal schism, dominating the Western Church since 1378, the voting was by nations (much as today voting would be by language groups); after news came of King Henry V of England decimating the French aristocracy at Agincourt, cooperation between French and English bishops in the council was as difficult as contemporary exchanges about beef trade. At Trent no voting was taken by national groups.

Henry VIII wanted to be master in his own house, and spoke of the English Church as "my church." The failure of Eugenius IV's council at Ferrara and Florence to achieve a union of East and West which could be sustained was explicitly noted by Henry as justifying his decision to have a Church Catholic but not controlled by the Bishop of Rome. In short, in the English psyche the Roman claim to jurisdiction became and remained the neuralgic point. Elizabeth's political success seemed to be a providential vindication of her religious position, which was remarkably close to Luther, especially in regard to belief in the Real Presence. She did not want to be dominated by France or Philip of Spain. The defeat of the Spanish fleet in 1588 was long regarded as proof that Protestantism was identifiable with the English cause. I was once sharply rebuked by an eminent scientist for ecumenical endeavors towards reconciliation with the Roman see; how could I do that, he asked, when the Spanish defeat of 1588 proved the Protestant cause to be right?

Early in the eighteenth century it could be said that the way to keep England Protestant was to keep the navy in good repair.[6] On the other hand, the English educated classes much admired the *Enchiridion* and other writings of Erasmus, and from him inherited the belief that excessive definition in dogma was undesirable. To read Erasmus is constantly to be saying to oneself, so that is where Anglican attitudes come from. He did not like Luther's breach with Rome or his polemic against the freedom of the will, profoundly indebted to Augustine's polemic against Julian of Eclanum.

The Thirty-Nine Articles, once influential, no longer have the authority for the Anglican Communion which they once enjoyed. That is partly because of great awareness of difficulties if they are to be reconciled with the more obviously Catholic liturgy of the Book of Common Prayer, partly because of their insufficiency and their dependence on the sixteenth-century context. In the early seventeenth century, for William Laud and others, they were already treated as articles of peace, not binding consciences. For Puritan Calvinists they initially looked more acceptable than the Prayer Book and the very Catholic language of the Ordinal, but article 16 was not at all Calvinist on the possibility of falling from grace, and article 17 on predestination was so broad as to be acceptable for Calvinist, Arminian, or Thomist. The Augustana prudently treats that subject as virtually secondary. Calvinist Puritans were very uncomfortable with article 20, that "the Church . . . has authority in controversies of faith."

On justification the Articles stand close to the Lutheran Confessions. "We are accounted righteous before God only for the merit of Christ by faith and not for our own works or deservings." "Although good works, which are the fruits of faith and follow after justification, cannot put away our sin . . . yet they are . . . acceptable to God in Christ. By them a lively faith may be known." "Works done before the grace of Christ . . . do not make men meet to receive grace or deserve grace of congruity." That proposition agrees with Trent.

It was surely realistic psychology when the Council of Trent spoke of preparatory disposition of the soul inclining towards faith. The first movement towards faith is seldom a lightning flash and thunderclap. However, for medieval schoolmen it was axiomatic that "virtues do not lead to faith, but faith to virtues."[7] But Trent made no definition about merit or either condignity or of congruity. The term merit is accepted at Trent in the sense of good works having moral value, not strictly the quid pro quo of desert. There was awareness of the text in the epistle to the Hebrews 6:10, "God is not so unjust as to overlook your work and love which you showed for his sake in serving the saints." In any event it is hardly possible to speak of condign merit except in relation to our Lord and his holy mother. The concept is more at home in a discussion of retribution in punishment.

The bishops and theologians at Trent feared Protestant language about absolute assurance (you are justified if you feel certain that you are). Anglicans were not so worried, but certainly did not want language indistinguishable from presumption on God's grace. The only point at which there is a rejoicing in assurance in the Prayer Book is in the postcommunion prayer thanking God for the assurance given by participation in Communion. The context is sacramental; it is not about a feeling. Cranmer's homily on salvation directly denies that faith can be the formal cause of justification.

Richard Hooker, like Luther in his commentary on the epistle to the Galatians, affirmed that the Roman Catholic Church has the true foundation, but has bits of superstructure that are mistaken. Bishop Davenant of Salisbury in 1631 strongly opposed the distinction between justification and sanctification when that distinction is understood as two different temporal stages in the growth of the soul. They are, he said, inseparable and contemporaneous. Bishop Forbes of Edinburgh (d. 1634) thought Cranmer less than correct in denying penitence to be integral to faith in justification. He agreed with Melanchthon that penitence is a condition of forgiveness. Forbes marveled at Suarez's wriggling when confronted by the notion of imputed righteousness. But in his view Bellarmine on justification wrote well except for the absurd assumption that all Protestants are antinomian libertines. He agreed with the Catholic Cassander that often disagreements were verbal more than real.

On the Protestant side the Tridentine decisions have commonly been regarded as sealing the split to make reconciliation insoluble. Among Anglicans we remember the saying of Sir Thomas Browne in his *Religio Medici* (1642) thanking God for being a member of the Church of England: "I condemn not all things in the Council of Trent, nor approve all in the Synod of Dort." (Browne had a Lutheran friend named Theodor Jonas from Iceland who visited him every year.)

To the Catholic eye of the great historian Jedin the root of the separation goes back to Luther's action in throwing *Exsurge Domine* into the fire. The sixteenth-century Lutherans did not want a new Church; yet they had acute difficulty with the jurisdiction of bishops, mainly for the practical reason that outside of Cologne they did not receive sympathy. That coolness was naturally reinforced after the Peasants' Revolt which made the Reformation look like a movement to overthrow authority, and led Luther to speak against the peasants. And the millennial excitements at Münster seemed to conservatives a nightmare. Was this what Reform was about?

When the Lutherans were invited to Trent, it was understandable that the council did not want to renegotiate matters already decided which had required months of discussion. Justification, which the Curia expected to need fifteen days, had needed a full seven months. The council was in no mood to listen to a case for Protestantism, responsible for war in Germany. Of course at the council unanimity was not easily achieved. Seripando, a general of the Augustinians, was often ill at ease with drafts from Spanish Jesuits, especially Laynez. Many at the council were alarmed by what Seripando or the English Reginald Pole, or Johannes Gropper, had to say about justification. One bishop said to Seripando that if he had his way, the world would groan to find itself Lutheran.[8] When Gropper arrived from Cologne, the bishop of Bologna was briefed to keep him in his place and answer him.[9] Debate on imputation of Christ's righteousness was strenuous. Seripando observed that the language was in Scripture, "I do not want it left in possession of the Lutherans.[10] Seripando had studied St. Thomas, and the Thomist ingredients to his thinking helped him to propose conciliatory wording.

John Henry Newman observed in his book on justification (1838) that the doctrine of imputed righteousness was closely akin to the doctrine of the sacrifice of the Mass. The believer prays, "Father, only look on us as found in him."

On both sides of the divide, justification is intimately bound up with sanctification. Acceptance before God is both remission and renewal, both forgiveness and recreation. Throughout the entire process the believer is under the grace and Spirit of Christ. In the *City of God*, Augustine declares that "we live our lives under forgiveness," and wrote the famous sentence (19, 27), "In this life our righteousness consists more in the forgiveness of sins than in perfection of virtues."

When we are thinking not of our learning now in Christ's school but of our prospects at death and at the final divine judgment, then all believers rely solely on the mercy of God. "On account of the uncertainty of the righteousness of our own deeds and the danger of vainglory, it is safer to rest our entire confidence exclusively upon the mercy and loving kindness of God."[11] Where justification is being considered in this eschatological context, human reliance is on the merits of Christ as our high priest pleading on our behalf, and in that context the language of imputation speaks to our condition. We put our trust in the belief that "the Father looking on us sees Christ in us."[12] "Rock of Ages" is a hymn I have seldom heard lately in Anglican churches, but more frequently at a Catholic Mass. "Nothing in my hand I bring, Simply to thy cross I cling."

In the twenty-first century it has become an effort for us to think ourselves back into the mind of our sixteenth-century forebears. Juridical categories no longer seem appropriate for expressing a relationship with our Maker marked by love. We might even wonder that a matter marked by such extreme intricacy as justification could be given as a reason for a momentous split in the Western Church which to our own time creates social tensions in Belfast or in Germany or in Australia. There could be questions how to justify the elevation of justification *sola fide sola gratia* to be the sole and supreme criterion of the authentic Gospel. We have come to think that in our time we are largely divided because we are divided. There remains a residuum of fear and withdrawal. To overcome the inertia of the past takes us back to Sisyphus and his boulder. Moreover, there remains an element derived from the radical wing of the Reformation in the notion that the quest for the one Church is an impractical ideal and a dangerous illusion.

The debate about justification is a quest for understanding what it is to be human. In varying ways Augustana and Trent and the Thirty-Nine Articles all follow in the wake of Augustine and his pessimistic diagnosis of human nature, a diagnosis which for us has been reinforced by Darwin, Marx, and Freud who in different degrees can be taken to underpin a conservative estimate of human corruption, contrasting with the optimistic account of humanity congenial to the Enlightenment or *Aufklärung*. Moreover, our historians no longer allow us to think of the medieval Western Church as essentially corrupt even if the documents of Trent itself show beyond doubt that there were serious problems. There were corruptions in those times; in human society there always are. Major Church tragedies today are poor, wounded Ireland and indifferent England and Scotland. But the system of Catholic piety and spirituality has produced saints as well as having room for corrupt prelates: Thomas à Kempis as well as Popes Alexander VI or Julius II, the saintly poor parson in Chaucer's *Canterbury Tales* as well as his unscrupulous pardoner selling bogus relics and indulgences.

Underlying the sixteenth-century debate lay the tension between the predestinarianism of Augustine, assumed by both Luther and John Calvin, and the affirmation of the freedom of the will. Even Augustine could concede that there is cooperation between the will and God's grace. "He who made you does not justify you without you."[13] The doctrines and canons of Trent on justification show anxiety to preserve free will and human cooperation. The Protestants preferred Augustine's writings against Julian of Eclanum. Augustine's biographer Possidius tells us that his candle could be seen burning far into the night as he composed his lengthy incomplete polemic against Julian. The Anglican John Burnaby, author of a classic intellectual biography very sympathetic to Augustine once commented to me that it would have been better if Augustine had gone to bed at half past ten.[14]

Notes

[1] Joseph Mede, *Works* (3rd edition, 1672) 863: "Often one sect of Religion condemns that in another which it self affirms because it understands not its own in another's terms and after another way."

[2] Wilhelm Mauer, *Historical Commentary on the Augsburg Confession*, trans. H. George Anderson (Philadelphia: Fortress Press, 1986) 194.

[3] Norman P. Tanner, S.J., ed., *Decrees of the Ecumenical Councils*, vol. II (London: Sheed and Ward and Washington: Georgetown University Press, 1990) 684. For later references to the Council of Trent, see the Tanner volume.

[4] Fisher, *English Works*, ed. J.E.B. Mayor, 1876, I 272, 274.

[5] *Concil. Trident.* VI/1, 201.18ff.; VII/1, 524 cf. 180 on Pope Julius III's failure to achieve curial reform in 1551.

[6] Addison, *The Spectator* iii 437, ed. Bond.

[7] Landgraf, *Domengeschichte des MA*, I, 2, p. 25.
[8] *CT* V 542ff.
[9] Sarpi ET 314.
[10] *CT* V 674.
[11] Bellarmine, *Justif.* 5, 7, ed. Rom. 1840, 886.
[12] Newman, *Justif.* 161.
[13] Augustine, *Sermo* 169.13.
[14] John Burnaby, *Amor Dei*, 2nd rev. ed. (London: Hodder & Stoughton, 1938).

Chapter 4

A Model for a New Joint Declaration: An Episcopalian Reaction to the *Joint Declaration on Justification*

R. William Franklin

Berkeley Divinity School and the Eucharistic Tradition

The Yale Conference on the *Joint Declaration on Justification* was sponsored by the Berkeley Divinity School at Yale as well as by the Divinity School of Yale University. As dean of Berkeley at the time of the conference, and now as dean emeritus, I want to add to Professor Chadwick's Anglican response the views of an American Episcopalian, particularly as they relate to the eucharistic tradition of the Berkeley Divinity School. My intention is to reflect on the relevance that tradition might have for a new "Joint Declaration" which might be signed by the Anglican Communion and the Roman Catholic Church. This essay applies the analysis derived from the Yale Conference on the *Joint Declaration on Justification* to Anglican-Roman Catholic relations as they have evolved to the end of the year 2002.

Professor George Lindbeck has reminded us that the contribution of the Yale Divinity School to the ecumenical movement has been "persons, ideas, and scholarship."[1] Berkeley's initial contribution to the ecumenical movement was more specific: the introduction of the liturgical movement into the Episcopal Church. This work was first begun under the person who served as dean of Berkeley from 1918 to 1941, William Palmer Ladd (1870–1941).

The liturgical movement in the Episcopal Church sought to restore the Eucharist to the heart of Christian worship and life by encouraging four reforms: (1) to give in the celebration of the Eucharist a more full and distinctive place for the ministry of the Word; (2) to restore to the Eucharist in a clear and unmistakable way what the Anglican Benedictine Dom Gregory Dix called the "fourfold shape" of the eucharistic action of the ancient and undivided Church; (3) to encourage the full and active participation in the Eucharist of all the people of God, as in the early Church; and finally, (4) as called for by Ladd, to allow for the flexibility of new eucharistic liturgies in the Episcopal Church, drawing on the resources of other Christian traditions, particularly that of the Roman Catholic Church and its own parallel liturgical movement as it was developing among French, German, and Belgian Benedictines.

From Berkeley Divinity School there emerged the first generation of scholars in the twentieth-century Episcopal Church who were engaged in the study, revision, and renewal of Christian liturgy and, in consequence, in the search for Christian unity. Among these persons were Massey Sheppard, Boone Porter, and Leonel Mitchell. Their liturgical scholarship transcended denominational divisions. These scholars from Berkeley contributed to the recovery of the ancient shape of the liturgy as reflected in the 1979 *Book of Common Prayer* (U.S.) and thus to the revival of the common ancient liturgical structure that all Christians share. They were deeply convinced that the twentieth-century convergence in the reform of worship, resulting from the liturgical movement, powerfully served the cause of Christian unity.

As a result of the parallel liturgical movement in the Roman Catholic Church and in other Provinces of the Anglican Communion, the underlying structures of the new Anglican and Roman Catholic eucharistic rites of the 1960s were almost identical. Further, with the adoption of the Revised Common Lectionary by the Provinces of the Anglican Communion (and other Christian traditions, including the Lutherans), Anglicans and Roman Catholics came to share a common approach to Scripture as prescribed for the Sundays of the Church year. These structures, texts, and lectionaries, which were similar to those of the post-Vatican II Roman Catholic Church, were key to the shape of the 1979 American Prayer Book and to the more recent revision and renewal of the liturgy of the Church of England. The liturgical scholarship emerging from Berkeley over several decades was clearly a factor which helped Anglicans and Roman Catholics to grow together toward unity. As bearer of this liturgical tradition and as a sponsor of the Yale Conference on Justification in 2000, it is appropriate for me, for four years dean at Berkeley, in this essay to call on Anglicans and Roman Catholics to produce a "Joint Declaration on the Eucharist" following the methodology of Lutherans and Roman Catholics in the *Joint Declaration on Justification*.

Anglicans and the *Joint Declaration on Justification*

Despite the fact that the doctrine of justification has not played the same or even a similar role within Anglicanism as within Lutheranism and Roman Catholicism, Anglican theologians and leaders welcomed the signing of the *Joint Declaration on the Doctrine of Justification* at Augsburg in 1999. For William Petersen, provost of Bexley Hall Episcopal Seminary, the declaration "is a sign-post and encouragement pointing to the goal of peace and unity" among the Churches.[2] For Henry Chadwick, of Oxford and the Church of England, "the consensus in the *Joint Declaration on Justification* is a remarkable millennial achievement by both parties to the discussion over several years."[3] Two other contributors to the present volume, Michael Root and Gabriel Fackre, raise the question of whether the *Joint Declaration* might become a multilateral agreement which Anglicans could sign. Root specifically writes: "the understanding of justification embodied in the declaration might prove capable of a wider affirmation. . . . If bilateral agreements are to enrich the total ecumenical movement, means need to be found to extend bilateral agreements beyond their original participants."[4] However, Root goes on to say, "how to effect such an extension is a tricky matter."[5] In the case of the Anglican Communion, I propose that rather than sign the *Joint Declaration on the Doctrine of Justification*, Anglicans and Roman Catholics should adopt the methodology of the *Joint Declaration* to produce a parallel document on an issue which has been more specifically at the heart of our divisions, the Eucharist.

One of the reasons the Anglican Communion does not need to sign the *Joint Declaration* is that in bilateral dialogues the two communions have already come to agreement on the issue of justification. The second round of the Episcopal-Lutheran conversations (LED II) made a specific statement "On Justification" as part of the 1981 *Lutheran-Episcopal Dialogue: Report and Recommendations*. The substance of this statement recognized sufficient agreement on faith and on justification to allow the two Churches to proceed to a period of "interim eucharistic fellowship" in 1982 and to full communion in 2000.[6]

The international Anglican-Roman dialogue (ARCIC) did not directly address the doctrine of justification in its first phase, 1971–81. But the dialogue in 1983 published a joint statement, "Salvation and the Church" which sought to examine the resolution of doctrinal issues between Anglicans and Roman Catholics in the realm of soteriology. Justification was an immediate focus of this 1983 study and the conclusion reached by the dialogue in ARCIC-II was this:

> Justification is not an area where any remaining differences of theological interpretation or ecclesiological emphasis, either within or between our communions, can justify continuing separation. . . . We believe that our two communions are agreed on the essential aspects of salvation and on the Church's role within it. We have also realized the central meaning and profound significance that the message of justification and sanctification, within the whole doctrine of salvation, continues to have for us today.[7]

The Background of IARCCUM

This proposal for a "Joint Declaration on the Eucharist" grows out of the recent evolution of the Anglican-Roman Catholic dialogue. In their "Common Declaration" of December 1996, John Paul II and the archbishop of Canterbury, George Carey, spoke of the necessity of a meeting of Anglican and Roman Catholic bishops to evaluate progress in relationships between the two Churches. The Lambeth Conference of 1998 endorsed such a meeting of bishops and proposed that it be held in 2000, "encouraging Provinces to respond to the invitation of the Archbishop of Canterbury to submit items for its agenda."[8] Thus from May 14 to 20, 2000, under the chairmanship of Edward Cardinal Cassidy of the Pontifical Council for Promoting Christian Unity and the archbishop of Canterbury, George Carey, pairs of Anglican and Roman Catholic bishops met in Mississauga, near Toronto, Canada. After reviewing thirty-five years of ecumenical dialogue between the two Churches, the bishops called for the creation of a new Joint Commission to oversee the next steps in Anglican-Roman Catholic relations so that they might develop in a positive direction.

The new commission is known as IARCCUM, the International Anglican-Roman Catholic Commission for Unity and Mission. The majority of its members are bishops and the Commission has been divided into three subgroups, one of which is to explore the possibility of a joint declaration which would formally express the degree of agreement that exists between the two Churches at the point of doctrine. The task of this declaration was defined in "Communion in Mission," the communiqué of the May 2000 meeting at Mississauga:

The first recommendation of our action plan is that a Joint Unity Commission be established. This Commission will oversee the preparation of the Joint Declaration of Agreement . . . We believe that now is the appropriate time for the authorities of our two communions to recognize and endorse a new stage of communion through the signing of a Joint Declaration of Agreement. This Agreement would set out: our shared goal of visible unity, an acknowledgement of the consensus in faith that we have reached. . . . Our two communions would be invited to celebrate this Agreement around the world.[9]

IARCCUM has now met on two occasions, November 20–24, 2001, and November 19–23, 2002. The second of these meetings reaffirmed the goals of "Communion in Mission":

1. The leaders of the two communions would sign a "Joint Declaration" which recognizes that a new level of communion has been achieved.
2. The Agreement would point to the goal of full visible unity.
3. The Agreement would declare that "a new stage of evangelical communion" has been reached between Anglicans and Roman Catholics.

I propose that at the heart of this "new stage of evangelical communion" there be a Joint Declaration on the Eucharist.

What IARCCUM Can Learn from
The Joint Declaration on Justification

An analysis of the process leading to the *Joint Declaration on Justification* reveals that there were seven stages that led to the production of the document, stages that IARCCUM should now follow in its work on the Eucharist:

(1) A period of theological study of many decades before the formal beginning of dialogue. The work of the official Lutheran-Roman Catholic dialogue was based on two generations of earlier scholarship on the doctrine of justification as Professor Lindbeck has outlined in the present volume.

(2) Publication of agreed statements on justification from official international and national dialogues. Five of these were particularly important: (a) the Malta Report of 1971 which laid out a program for considering the doctrine of justification; (b) the 1972 Report of the Joint Lutheran-Roman Catholic Study Commission, *The Gospel and the Church*; (c) the 1983 document *Justification by Faith* produced by the United States Roman Catholic-Lutheran Dialogue; (d) the 1986 German volume published in 1990 in English as *The Condemnations of the*

Reformation Era: Do They Still Divide?[10]; and (e) the 1994 document of the international dialogue, *Church and Justification*, which concluded that there were no longer any Church-dividing issues over justification.

(3) Realization that these documents had no official status in the Churches. It became clear that though the documents produced by these commissions had been the work of official representatives of the Churches, the documents themselves had no official status and were not making a concrete impact on the practical life of the Churches. In light of this reality, the Lutheran World Federation and the Pontifical Council for Promoting Christian Unity formed a new special Lutheran-Roman Catholic Dialogue Commission with the specific task of framing a "Joint Declaration on the Doctrine of Justification." The new departure here was that the Churches themselves and not just their theologians would be asked officially to declare that consensus had been reached.

(4) Submission to Lutherans. In February 1997 the *Joint Declaration* was submitted to the Churches of the Lutheran World Federation for approval, and in June 1998 the Federation was able to reach an almost unanimous response from its member Churches in favor of the declaration.

(5) Submission to Roman Catholics. In the Roman Catholic Church final approval was entrusted to the Pontifical Council for Promoting Christian Unity in close consultation with the Congregation for the Doctrine of the Faith. On June 25, 1998, the Pontifical Council was able to announce that, after the production of some additional commentaries and explanations, a consensus had been reached on the document.

(6) Nature of the Document Signed on October 31, 1999: (a) it ratifies thirty years of dialogue; (b) justification is placed within the framework of a trinitarian and christological confession of faith; (c) the mutual condemnations are lifted and seen as no longer Church-dividing; and (d) the document is a "differentiated consensus," not a "total agreement," which opens the way for resolution of other differences.

(7) Three results of the declaration which point to the future: (a) it legislatively affirms a new level of communion between the two Churches; (b) it opens the way for a more intense life together at the local level; and (c) it lays the groundwork for attacking the remaining issues that must be faced before full communion between the Roman Catholic Church and the Lutheran Churches can be achieved.

These three historic points of achievement were restated and underlined by Pope John Paul II in an address to a delegation from the Lutheran Church of Norway visiting Rome on November 16, 2002: "We are committed to moving further ahead on the path to reconciliation. The 'Joint Declaration on the Doctrine of Justification' between the Lutheran World Federation and the Catholic Church, signed in 1999, paves the way for more extensive common witness. It brings us a step closer to the full visible unity which is the goal of our dialogue."[11]

The Model for IARCCUM

IARCCUM can follow exactly these seven stages in producing a declaration on the Eucharist:

(1) A period of theological study of many decades before the beginning of formal dialogue. It can be argued that the Eucharist occupies the place in Anglican-Roman Catholic relations that justification holds between Lutherans and Catholics. This is because Pope Leo XIII in *Apostolicae Curae* (1896) laid out a doctrinal basis for Roman Catholic rejection of the validity of Anglican ministry. At the heart of *Apostolicae Curae* is the argument that by omission of any reference to the Eucharist as a sacrifice in the 1552 *Book of Common Prayer*, the Church of England intended to introduce a radically new rite, markedly different from those approved by the Roman Catholic Church, and thus irrevocably broke its link to Catholic tradition.

Yet from the sixteenth century the Church of England attempted to contain in a positive sense both Catholic and Protestant affirmations about the Eucharist. More specifically, in the nineteenth century E. B. Pusey, one of the leaders of the Oxford Movement, fostered a eucharistic revival founded on an exegesis of patristic texts for Anglicans which documented the gradual evolution of an understanding of the Eucharist as a sacrifice. By the late nineteenth century, for one group of Anglicans "the Catholic conception of the . . . sacraments had at last come into its own."[12] The promulgation of Vatican II's Decree on Ecumenism, *Unitatis redintegratio* (1964), which recognized but did not define the "special place" of Anglicanism among the Churches of the West, opened the way for a dialogue which could now officially take up theological issues on the Eucharist which had been at the heart of Leo XIII's 1896 condemnation of Anglican orders.

(2) Creation of international and national dialogues that have taken up the topic of the Eucharist. The first Anglican-Roman Catholic International Commission (ARCIC-I) ended its work in 1981 with the publication of its *Final Report* in which theological convergence was registered by representatives of the two Churches on the specific issue

which Leo XIII had said was at the heart of division: the essentials of eucharistic faith with regard to the sacramental presence of Christ and the sacrificial dimension of the Eucharist itself. Anglicans at the 1988 Lambeth Conference officially recognized the agreed statements of ARCIC-I on eucharistic doctrine and their elucidations as "constant in substance with the faith of Anglicans."[13]

However, in its *Response to the Final Report* of 1991, the Vatican, while approving the main thrust of the ARCIC statement on eucharistic doctrine, asked for clarifications concerning four points: (1) the link of the eucharistic memorial with the sacrifice of Calvary; (2) the propitiatory nature of the eucharistic sacrifice; (3) certitude that Christ is present sacramentally; and (4) adoration of Christ in the reserved sacrament.

In the light of this Vatican response, ARCIC-II published in 1993 its *Clarifications of Certain Aspects of the Agreed Statements on Eucharist and Ministry* and ARC-USA published in 1994 *Five Affirmations on the Eucharist as Sacrifice*. The American *Affirmations* conclude: "the Eucharist as a sacrifice is not an issue that divides our two Churches."[14] This judgment was confirmed by the Pontifical Council for Christian Unity in a letter of Cardinal Cassidy of March 11, 1994, to the co-chairpersons of ARCIC-II in response to their *Clarifications*: "The agreement reached on the Eucharist . . . by ARCIC-I is thus greatly strengthened and no further study would seem to be required at this stage."[15]

Nevertheless, in statements published from 1995 to 2001, the Roman Congregation for the Doctrine of the Faith has continued to cast doubt on the level of consensus achieved on the Eucharist and even at the national level throughout the world reception of consensus on the Eucharist remains irregular. For example, in 1998 the three Roman Catholic Bishops' Conferences of England and Wales, Ireland, and Scotland published *One Bread One Body*, a firm restatement of Roman Catholic discipline against eucharistic sharing with Anglicans. The House of Bishops of the Church of England in 2001 responded to that statement with *The Eucharist: Sacrament of Unity*. This passage by the Anglican bishops summarizes the deficit in respect to reception of the eucharistic consensus at the national level in Great Britain: "*One Bread One Body* makes explicit a number of erroneous assumptions by the Roman Catholic Church about the Church of England, the Reformation, Anglican teaching regarding the eucharistic sacrifice and the presence of Christ in the sacrament. . . . We take this opportunity to correct these misapprehensions."[16]

**Only a "Joint Declaration on the Eucharist"
Can Solve This Widespread Misunderstanding**

Confusion concerning the Eucharist in England, homeland of the Anglican-Roman Catholic schism, merely mirrors in microcosm the level of ignorance on eucharistic congruence that prevails around the world. Despite the agreed texts of theological commissions on the Eucharist, these texts have not been officially "received" by the Churches, nor does pastoral practice at local, diocesan, or national levels reflect the consensus reached by the agreements. Thus we have reached the stage where the only way forward is a joint declaration by Anglicans and Roman Catholics based on the model of the *Joint Declaration on the Doctrine of Justification.*

Stages one and two of the *Joint Declaration* process have been reached already with regard to the Eucharist. With the creation of IARCCUM, stage three has now also been reached. The document to be produced by IARCCUM should follow the outline of the 1999 *Joint Declaration on Justification*:

(1) The document should begin with ratification of the Churches' thirty years of dialogue and agreement on these specific points: (a) affirming that in the Eucharist the Church makes present the sacrifice of Calvary; (b) affirming that Christ in the Eucharist makes himself present sacramentally; and (c) affirming that the Body and Blood of Christ may be reserved for the sick and that Christ may be adored in the reserved sacrament.

(2) Agreement on the Eucharist should be placed within the broader context of affirming together the essentials of the Christian faith, and here the four points of the Chicago-Lambeth Quadrilateral (1886, 1888) might provide the outline: (a) the Holy Scriptures; (b) the creeds; (c) the two sacraments of baptism and the Eucharist; (d) the historic episcopate.

(3) In parallel to the *Joint Declaration on Justification* and its lifting of the sixteenth-century Lutheran and Roman Catholic condemnations, the IARCCUM document should find some means of removing the nineteenth-century Roman Catholic condemnation of Anglican orders.

(4) The IARCCUM text by following the *Joint Declaration on Justification* in affirming "differentiated consensus" rather than "total agreement" on the Eucharist could open the way to the sharing of one doctrine of the Eucharist while at this time not attempting to solve the issue of the role of women in presiding at the Eucharist.

Additionally, I propose that the legislative process of the 1999 *Joint Declaration on Justification* be followed. A parallel process to step four of the consideration of justification would be submission of the IARCCUM text to each Province of the Anglican Communion for ratification, rather than to the Lambeth Conference for its approval in 2008. Also, a parallel to step five of the Joint Declaration process would be submission of the document to the Roman Pontifical Council for Promoting Christian Unity and to the Roman Congregation for the Doctrine of the Faith to insure that Rome speaks henceforth with one authoritative voice on this key issue of eucharistic doctrine, thereby diminishing the confusion in comprehending the mind of Rome on this matter which has marked the last five years.

There would be three consequences to an official signing of the IARCCUM text:

(1) The solemn occasion would symbolize the fact that a new level of communion had been reached, an ecumenical milestone from which there could be no turning back.

(2) A "Declaration" would insure that local pastoral practice adheres to the mind of the two Churches on eucharistic doctrine and practice.

(3) Impetus would be given to resolving the outstanding issues blocking the path to the goal of full visible unity, particularly the question of the role of women in ordained ministry.

The significance of the *Joint Declaration on the Doctrine of Justification* of 1999 for the ecumenical movement as a whole, therefore, is that it establishes a new pattern of a series of "Declarations" to be signed by the Churches at their highest levels of authority, a pattern which would aid the continuation of progress toward Christian unity. A year after delivering at Yale the paper included in this volume, Cardinal Walter Kasper gave the Dudleian Lecture at Harvard University. The cardinal, happy to be fulfilling his old vocation as professor, told his hearers that what is required for ecumenism now is political skill, able communication, energy, and patience to translate the neglected documents of the bilateral dialogues of the past three decades into the lifeblood of the Churches. He said that it would take a new generation of ecumenical leaders to accomplish this task and thus he issued the following charge to the students of Harvard, even as the papers in the present volume were delivered to students of the Yale and Berkeley Divinity Schools:

> These documents [of the bilaterals of the past thirty years] are the work of ecumenical experts and do not speak on behalf of the Churches them-

selves. . . . They must become flesh in the Churches. This is, or can be, a long and complicated process, involving not only the authorities in the Churches, but also the life and the hearts of the faithful. . . . This process requires determination, but also patience, which is according to the New Testament a fundamental attitude of Christian hope and according to Peguy the little sister of hope. Patience as the sister of hope is the true strength of Christian faith.[17]

Kasper's mission was also the mission of William Palmer Ladd at the Berkeley Divinity School, exercised patiently over a period of twenty-three years, forming a generation of Episcopal leaders whose "new views mediated through traditional patterns,"[18] to use a phrase of Cardinal Kasper, would profoundly affect the future and allow the Episcopal Church to build spiritual ties to other Churches through the constant celebration of a Eucharist renewed and enriched by the great wide Christian tradition that expands our narrow denominational boundaries toward a future horizon of endless spiritual possibility.

Notes

[1] George Lindbeck, "The University and Ecumenism," *Justification and the Future of the Ecumenical Movement* (Collegeville: Liturgical Press, 2003) 6.

[2] William H. Petersen, "The Lutheran-Roman Catholic Joint Declaration on the Doctrine of Justification. Soteriological and Ecclesiological Implications from an Anglican Perspective," *Journal of Ecumenical Studies* 38 (2001) 52.

[3] Henry Chadwick, "An Anglican Reaction: Across the Reformation Divide," *Justification and the Future of the Ecumenical Movement* (Collegeville: Liturgical Press, 2003) 23.

[4] Michael Root, "The Implications of the *Joint Declaration on Justification* and Its Wider Impact for Lutheran Participation in the Ecumenical Movement," *Justification and the Future of the Ecumenical Movement* (Collegeville: Liturgical Press, 2003) 50.

[5] Ibid.

[6] Petersen, "The Lutheran-Roman Catholic Joint Declaration on the Doctrine of Justification," 50–63.

[7] "Salvation and the Church" in Jeffrey Gros, Harding Meyer, and William G. Rusch, eds., *Growth in Agreement II: Reports and Agreed Statements of Ecumenical Conversations 1982-1998*, Faith and Order Paper 187 (Geneva: WCC Publications and Grand Rapids, Mich.: Eerdmans, 2000) 315–25; cf. also Martin E. Brinkman, "Justification in Two Other Dialogues" in *Justification in Ecumenical Dialogue* (Utrecht: Interuniversity Institute for Missiology and Ecumenical Research, 1996) 169–201, and ibid., "Justification and Ecumenical Dialogue in *Sacraments of Freedom* (Meinema: Zottermeer, 1999) 125–52.

[8] "Called to be One: Section IV Report," in Mark Dyer et al., eds., *The Official Report of the Lambeth Conference 1998* (Harrisburg, Pa.: Morehouse, 1999) 256.

[9] "Communion in Mission," (Mississauga, Canada, May 19, 2000) 2–3; cf. also *Information Service of the Pontifical Council for Promoting Christian Unity*, 1081 (2001, iv) 154–56.

[10] Lehmann, Karl and Wolfhart Pannenberg, eds. *The Condemnations of the Reformation Era: Do They Still Divide,* trans. Margaret Kohl (Minneapolis: Fortress Press, 2000); cf. also Lehmann, Karl, Michael Root, and William G. Rusch, *Justification by Faith: Do the Sixteenth-Century Condemnations Still Apply?* trans. Michael Root and William G. Rusch (New York: Continuum, 1997).

[11] John Paul II, *L'Osservatore Romano* (November 17, 2002) 5.

[12] A. G. Hebert, *Intercommunion* (London: SPCK, 1932) vii.

[13] The full text of the Lambeth resolution can be found in *Ecumenical Bulletin* (Nov.–Dec. 1988) 19–21.

[14] R. William Franklin, "ARC-USA: Five Affirmations on the Eucharist as Sacrifice," *Worship* 69, 5 (1995) 389–90.

[15] Letter of Edward Cardinal Cassidy to the co-chairpersons of ARCIC-II, March 11, 1994 (#12781941e).

[16] House of Bishops of the Church of England, *The Eucharist: Sacrament of Unity* (London: Church Publishing House, 2001) vii–viii.

[17] Walter Kasper, "The Nature and Purpose of Ecumenical Dialogue," *Harvard University Divinity School Bulletin* (Winter 2001–02) 22.

[18] Ibid., 22.

Chapter 5

The Implications of the
Joint Declaration on Justification
and Its Wider Impact for Lutheran
Participation in the Ecumenical Movement[1]

Michael Root

The topic I have been assigned is broad. It does not directly concern the doctrine of justification, but rather the implications of the recent *Joint Declaration on the Doctrine of Justification* and the process that has surrounded it for Lutheran participation in the ecumenical movement. How does the *Joint Declaration* affect the way Lutherans interact with others in the search for the greater visible unity of the Church? Thus, the bulk of this essay will focus less on justification than on the present agreement on justification.

I will first discuss how I believe the agreement on justification achieved in the *Joint Declaration* should change the way Lutherans and others think about justification. In the second half of the presentation, I will discuss how the present agreement fits into wider changes in Lutheran participation in the ecumenical movement.

I. The Agreement on Justification

The *Joint Declaration* is not just an agreement on justification between the Lutheran and Catholic Churches; it is also an agreement among Lutherans on how rightly to state the doctrine of justification. The doctrine of justification as expressed in the *Joint Declaration* is not defined as the only adequate way to state a Reformation doctrine of justification, but its ratification by the Lutheran Churches implies that it represents at least one adequate way to state the doctrine of justification.

The precise authority of this decision is not altogether clear. The *Joint Declaration* is not a new confessional text, but its ratification by the Churches does give it a certain weight.

This intra-Lutheran agreement is worth stressing. While Lutherans have consistently insisted that the doctrine of justification is "the chief article in the Christian life," as Melanchthon put it in the Augsburg Confession (20:8), Lutherans have also vehemently argued with one another over just what is a correct statement of that doctrine. The internal debates that almost split Lutheranism in the decades following Luther's death were for the most part debates over details of the doctrine of justification. The settlement that occurred in 1577 in the Formula of Concord was achieved only because of the exclusion of one side of the argument—the more radical Philippists—following the so-called Crypto-Calvinist controversy.

These intra-Lutheran debates have not been unique. It may be the case that the doctrine of justification as it has been debated in Western Christianity has within it an inherent instability. In the century following the Reformation division, the Reformed and Roman Catholic traditions also underwent controversies related to justification that almost proved Church-dividing: the Arminian controversy among the Reformed and the *de auxiliis* controversy among Catholics. Because the doctrine of justification is more defining for Lutherans than for other traditions, any inherent instability in this doctrine tends to be more unsettling for Lutherans, however, than for others.

In the twentieth century, Lutherans suffered a major embarrassment at the 1963 Assembly of the Lutheran World Federation in Helsinki when they proved unable to agree on a prepared statement on "Justification Today." The *Joint Declaration* in a sense has redeemed that failure (although it should be noted that the task in the *Joint Declaration* was easier, precisely because the question of how to express the doctrine in a way that might be more relevant to contemporary humanity was not addressed). The intra-Lutheran agreement in the *Joint Declaration* was not achieved without effort. The Lutheran Churches in Germany and Finland produced the most detailed critiques of the 1995 draft of the *Joint Declaration,* and they were each asked to appoint a representative to the drafting team that produced the last two revisions of the text. The Finnish and German concerns about the early draft often pulled in divergent directions and required careful mediation in formulating the Lutheran paragraphs in section 4 of the *Joint Declaration.* Some of the more lengthy and clumsy sections of the *Joint*

Declaration, most notably §29 on *simul justus et peccator* and concupiscence, were a result of this mediation effort.

On the whole, however, I believe this mediation effort was successful. In my estimation, the *Joint Declaration* preserves what is essential to a Reformation understanding of justification: that the righteousness of the Christian before God is not our work, but a gift of grace that comes to us in the Gospel proclaimed by Word and Sacrament; that this righteousness is and remains the righteousness of Christ in which the Christian participates by faith (the *extra nos* character of our justification); that this righteousness is complete and perfect, even while the old person lives within us in such a way that we do not fulfill the central commandment to love God with all our heart, mind, and strength (the *simul iustus et peccator*).

The *Joint Declaration* avoids a merely external and forensic understanding of justification both by stressing the inseparability of justification and the comprehensive renewal of the Christian and by understanding faith as itself unity with Christ and thus itself a form of regeneration. Paragraph 26 is here instructive. It states: "According to Lutheran understanding, God justifies the sinner in faith alone (*sola fide*). In faith they place their trust wholly in their Creator and Redeemer and thus live in communion with him" [the German is here perhaps more emphatic—*und ist so in Gemeinschaft mit ihm,* i.e., with God]. Life in communion with God is not something separable from faith. Faith *is* communion with God. Faith is thus itself regeneration. As §26 continues, "Because God's act [in effecting faith in the believer] is a new creation, it affects all dimensions of the person and leads to a new life in hope and love." This passage does refer to a life in hope and love as something that follows from God's act of effecting faith, but that act itself is said to be transformative. In the attempt to say that the transformation of the believer does not constitute the believer's righteousness before God, Lutherans have sometimes given the impression that justification is not itself or essentially a transformation, but that transformation is only a necessary but distinct consequence. The Lutheran understanding as represented in the *Joint Declaration* returns to the more classical and confessional Lutheran emphasis on faith as itself regeneration, even if that regeneration is not itself the Christian's righteousness. In Article 4 of the Apology to the Augsburg Confession, the longest and most detailed discussion of justification in the Lutheran Confessions, Melanchthon regularly equated the terms "justification" and "regeneration." As he stated in what amounts to a definition of justification: "'to be justified' means to make just persons out of unjust ones or to regenerate them, as well as to be pronounced or reckoned righteous" (Apol. IV.72). Later the Formula of Concord sought carefully to distinguish justification from the ongoing renewal that results from the struggle with sin, but it did not deny Melanchthon's equation of justification and regeneration: "For when the Holy Spirit has brought a person to faith and has justified that person, a regeneration has indeed taken place because he has transformed a child of wrath into a child of God and has translated the person from death into life" (SD III.20).

A significant aspect of the ecumenical achievement of the *Joint Declaration* is the way it faithfully states the Reformation understanding of justification while attending to worries that Catholics have often had about that understanding. Herein also lies some of the promise of the declaration for a wider agreement. Precisely in mediating both the Catholic and Lutheran differing emphases and the differing emphases within Lutheranism, the understanding of justification embodied in the declaration might prove capable of a wider affirmation. A multilateral agreement on justification is an interesting prospect. If bilateral agreements are to enrich the total ecumenical movement, means need to be found to extend bilateral agreements beyond their original participants. How to effect such an extension is a tricky matter, as has been discovered in Europe in attempts to extend the Lutheran-Reformed-United *Leuenberg Agreement* and the Anglican-German Evangelical *Meissen Agreement* to other Churches.

The difficulties involved are, however, not insuperable. If the ecumenical movement seeks a common witness to the Gospel on the basis of our shared faith, then a widely accepted official statement on justification, on that doctrine which Catholics and Lutherans now together say "directs us in a special way towards the heart of the New Testament witness to God's saving action in Christ" (§17), could be an ecumenical accomplishment of more than merely ecumenical importance.

But if the *Joint Declaration* is the success that I claim, then why has it proved so controversial among a relatively small minority of Lutherans in this country, but a much more sizable and prominent minority of Lutherans in Germany? While all but one of the German Lutheran *Landeskirchen* endorsed the *Joint Declaration*, many did so only after vehement debate and often with extended (and somewhat tortured) commentary on their decision. A minority of theology professors remain opposed to the *Joint Declaration*. What is the significance of this dissent for the ecumenical import of the *Joint Declaration*?

As I have noted, the doctrine of justification has been defining for Lutherans, especially for Lutheran theologians. A disagreement over justification can thus never be a trivial matter for Lutherans. In the case of the debate over the *Joint Declaration*, however, a particular dynamic of contemporary Lutheranism has become evident. Various commentators (most notably George Lindbeck and David Yeago) have sought to describe the polarization that has occurred in American Lutheranism in relation most clearly to ecumenical issues. Lindbeck has named the two poles "radical Lutherans" and "evangelical Catholics," or, alternatively in a description I still find illuminating, "denominational Lutherans" and "movement Lutherans." A variant of that polarization occurs among Lutherans at the world level over the doctrine of justification. This polarization concerns not just the doctrine of justification, but also is expressed in two differing understandings of the nature of the Reformation.

On one side stands the tradition of Luther scholarship most clearly represented by Gerhard Ebeling and in this country by Gerhard Forde, with roots both in the Luther renaissance of the early twentieth century and in dialectical theology, especially its more Bultmannian and Heideggerian side. As David Yeago has noted, a series of analogous dichotomies are here definitive—Law/Gospel; letter/spirit; human action/divine action; works/faith. Each dichotomy represents a mutually exclusive pair: Law or Gospel, human action or divine action, work or faith. These dichotomies are taken to be "the prime structuring principle which bounds and orders the conceptual space within which the coherence of Christian belief must be thought out."[2] For such a view, the mere assertion of these dichotomies is not enough; they must be seen to be determinative of that which is truly Christian. Otherwise, one has fallen into some subtle form of sub-Christian legalism.

Two further aspects of this sort of understanding of justification need be noted. First, since these dichotomies are taken to be determinative of the content of Christian faith, their absence in medieval and patristic theology and practice implies that the Reformation is not to be understood as a corrective movement within a continuous catholic tradition, but as a radical break, as a return to the pure sources after centuries of simple error: "*post tenebras lux,*" as the Reformation monument in Geneva prominently states. Second, the particular way the human member of the analogous dichotomies—Law, letter, human action, works—is identified with form and history makes any theological, and not just pragmatic, valuation of the Church in its historically embodied form difficult at best and always suspect. To use one of Gerhard Forde's favorite similes, an institution such as the ministry of the Church is to be like the instruction tape the heroes receive at the beginning of each episode of *Mission: Impossible*; it destroys itself as soon as its message is delivered. The Church is only the Church when, like a true symbol for Tillich, it is in the process of self-cancellation.

A second, alternative understanding of justification has its roots especially in the ecumenical dialogues. It differs not only in how the Reformation dichotomies are to be understood in detail, but also in the role of such dichotomies in the understanding of the Christian faith. The dichotomies are themselves to be understood within the larger context of the overarching narrative of creation and redemption confessed by the Church. Law and Gospel do not form a mutually exclusive pair which structures all Christian discourse, but are to be understood in the context of an ambiguous situation, in which the inherently good law is deformed by human sin and made into an opponent of God's good intention. Law and Gospel are a mutually exclusive pair in one context, but that context is not solely determinative of the entirety of Christian faith and life. This contextualization of the dichotomies permits a different reading of the relation of the Reformation to medieval and patristic theology. The Reformation is not forced into a situation of thorough discontinuity. In addition, the intrahistorical reality of the Church is not immediately devalued.

This description of the polarity in Lutheran thinking on justification is crude, but I hope it can indicate the problem the *Joint Declaration* faced and faces. Both strands of contemporary Lutheran thinking on justification are woven into the declaration. The presence of an entire section on "Law and Gospel" in section 4 is indicative. The earlier German study of the condemnations of the sixteenth century included no section on Law and Gospel for the straightforward reason that no relevant condemnations of either Church directly relate to Law and Gospel. This absence, however, elicited much criticism, especially from those for whom this dichotomy is not only essential, but comprehensively definitive. Thus, every draft of the *Joint Declaration* included such a section.

The difficulty with the mediation achieved in the *Declaration* is that, while the latter, more "ecumenical" reading of justification can accept such a mediation, the former, more dialectical reading has an inherent difficulty accepting any mediation of its outlook with any other. To mediate these comprehensive, definitive, and mutually exclusive dichotomies with some other perspective is to rob them of their comprehensive and definitive character, no matter how adequately and skillfully the details of this more dialectical position are taken up. The very enterprise of mediation must be suspect. No matter how skillful the mediation, it must fail from such a perspective. I believe a significant amount of the confusing and strikingly imprecise debate over paragraph 18 of the declaration and its statement that the doctrine of justification is "an indispensable criterion" of the Church's teaching and practice has been rooted in a perspective for which any mediation of its perspective with any other perspective is betrayal.

Nevertheless, the continuing existence of a debate within Lutheranism over the *Joint Declaration* must not obscure for us the theological and ecclesial achievement it represents.

Let me now ask what are the implications of the declaration for Lutheran participation in discussions about justification and salvation. What difference should the declaration make precisely for how Lutherans think about justification?

This is a more difficult question than it might seem. Lutheran thinking about justification has been contrastive. We have defined much of our understanding of justification over against what we have taken to be Catholic doctrine. The *Joint Declaration* does not claim to remove all Lutheran-Catholic differences over justification. The seven subsections of section 4 of the declaration make these remaining differences clear. Nevertheless, the declaration does put these differences in a new context, the context of a common confession of basic truths of the doctrine of justification. What should be the implications of this new contextualization of the doctrine of justification?

Most importantly, this new context should mean a move beyond an essentially contrastive understanding, a move beyond an understanding in which the identity of a Reformation understanding of justification is defined by its opposition to Roman Catholic teaching. In my own experience teaching the Lutheran Confessions postdeclaration, I have noticed how difficult it is to explain a Reformation understanding of justification without creating a Catholic straw man as a contrast figure. What would a noncontrastive understanding of justification be? Let me note three desiderata.

First, a noncontrastive yet Lutheran understanding of justification should be able to take seriously the call of the *Joint Declaration* to hear both the Lutheran and Catholic condemnations of the sixteenth century as "'salutary warnings' to which we must attend in our teaching and practice" (§42). In the 1980's German study of these condemnations, from which the phrase "salutary warnings" was taken, it is explicitly said that the condemnations are warnings "both for the members of the churches in which they were originally formulated and for members of the other Christian confession in question."[3] That study emphasized the need to take the condemnations as warnings against forms of speech that would lead to a renewal of now surmounted antitheses. But can we go a step further? Can Lutherans hear the condemnations of Trent as warnings against ways of stating justification by grace through faith that are easily misunderstood or as warnings about dangerous tendencies in the way they speak about justification, even if these dangers are ones that cannot always be avoided? Karl Barth once said that truly Pauline theology is always walking on the brink of heresy.[4] Even if that is so, it is all the more important to understand whether one is walking on the brink of heresy or has already stepped over it. When one is walking on the edge of a cliff, the difference of a few feet is nontrivial.

Lutherans should admit that a Reformation understanding of justification requires a balance that is not easily preserved. Arguments among Lutherans over how rightly to relate faith and works, justification and sanctification, go back at least to the Saxon visitation of the late 1520s. Günther Gassmann and Scott Hendrix say in their recent textbook on the Confessions: "As soon as evangelical pastors stepped into the pulpit, they began to complain that people misunderstood justification by faith to mean they no longer had to repent, obey the Commandments, or do good works. To prevent this misunderstanding is a main goal of the confessions, and this goal influences to a large extent how they speak about the Christian life."[5] Can Lutherans hear a salutary warning even in the condemnations of Trent related to merit (26 and 32)? Is there here a salutary warning to Lutherans not to neglect the reality toward which the concept of merit is meant to point, the "holiness without which no one will see the Lord (Heb 12:14)," the fit that will exist between eschatological perfection and the kingdom of heaven? A test of the impact of the *Joint Declaration* on Lutheran participation in the ecumenical movement will be whether Lutherans can learn to hear in Trent such salutary warnings.

A second, correlative aspect of a noncontrastive understanding of justification would be a much greater openness on the part of Lutherans to learn from non-Lutherans precisely in the area of the doctrine of justification. The *Joint Declaration* does not mean that we are now ready to produce a truly post-Reformation doctrine of justification, a teaching that would draw easily from Luther and Aquinas, Barth and Rahner, Jüngel and von Balthasar. It does mean, however, that we should be thinking toward such an understanding. As long as Lutheranism remains a distinct movement within the Church Catholic, one should expect Lutherans to draw on Luther more than, say, Aquinas, but can we move toward the point where Lutherans can draw on Catholic figures at least to the degree that some recent Catholic theologians have been able to draw on Luther? The road to the *Joint Declaration* was smoothed by the work of such Catholic Luther scholars as Otto Hermann Pesch and Peter Manns. A Catholic Luther scholar, Jared Wicks, was a member of the team that produced the last two versions of the declaration. Through the work of such scholars, Catholic theology has been enriched by the Reformation. Has Lutheran theology been enriched in the same way by Catholic sources? Or, if it has been so, has it been willing to acknowledge such enrichment? Lutheran Aquinas scholarship has been intermittent and not widely received by Lutheran theologians. Signs of improvement can be found in this regard, e.g., the subtle use of Aquinas in recent work by Bruce Marshall;[6] but we are still far from a truly creative, rather than simply contrastive, Lutheran engagement with the Catholic tradition.

Third, a noncontrastive Lutheran approach to justification will need to take seriously the question of corporate repentance for what we have done with that doctrine. Has the doctrine of justification, even a formally correct doctrine of justification, been used more as a means of ratifying division than as a proclamation of the Gospel? Has it been used as what Ephraim Radner calls a "contrastive identifier," a means to mark off ourselves as the true Church from the heretical opposition?[7] However one may judge the theological issues of the Reformation, it appears that at some point a will to division set in that helped to assure that theological reconciliation would not occur. Does even a correct doctrine of justification justify the self-sufficiency that has often ruled Lutheran self-understanding?

Moving toward such a noncontrastive understanding of justification is not an easy or risk-free matter. Lutheran self-understanding has generally dwelt within more sheltered surroundings. But the alternative in the present situation is a sectarian version of the Reformation, however sophisticated.

One question, then, for the postdeclaration context of Lutheran ecumenism is: What are the implications of the present agreement for the way Lutherans have thought about the doctrine of justification? The implications of the declaration will be limited if its relation to how

Lutherans think about justification remains merely external, if it does not call upon Lutherans to rethink how they have gone about understanding and presenting the doctrine of justification by grace through faith for the sake of Jesus Christ.

II. The Wider Ecumenical Context

The *Joint Declaration* was not signed in an ecumenical vacuum. It is not the sole ecumenical change for Lutherans in recent years. On the one hand, the rapprochement achieved between Lutherans and Reformed in Europe through the *Leuenberg Agreement* of 1973 has now been matched by the establishment of full communion between the Evangelical Lutheran Church in America and three Reformed Churches. The affirmation of the *Leuenberg Agreement* by the Church of Norway is another sign of progress in Lutheran-Reformed relations. On the other hand, Lutherans and Anglicans in Northern Europe, Canada, and the United States have been able to develop agreements which permit the immediate full recognition of ordained ministries, along with the acceptance by the Lutheran Churches of episcopal succession as one sign of the unity and continuity of the Church. When the *Joint Declaration* is placed alongside these other ecumenical developments, a complex and challenging picture develops.

If the doctrine of justification is no longer in itself a Church-dividing issue between Lutherans and Roman Catholics and if the classical differences between Lutheran and Reformed on such issues as the Lord's Supper and Christology are now settled, then the nexus of issues centered on ecclesiology, ministry, and authority in the Church becomes ever more central in ecumenical discussions.

The agreements with Catholics, Anglicans, and Reformed not only place a new emphasis on issues of ecclesiology, ministry, and authority, but they also change the institutional context in which Lutherans approach such issues. If the Lutheran-Anglican agreements in the U.S. and Canada are ratified, as seems likely, about 40 percent of the Lutherans in the world will be in churches which have accepted some form of episcopal succession. A Lutheran reception of episcopal succession has changed from being a theoretical possibility realized only in Sweden and Finland to being a possibility realized or in the process of being realized for two-fifths of contemporary Lutheranism. This shift inevitably will have some impact on how Lutherans engage issues of ecclesiology and ministry in the ecumenical setting.

Crucial for this shift has been the development of a more comprehensive and flexible understanding of apostolicity and ministry in such ecumenical texts as the Faith and Order study *Baptism, Eucharist and Ministry* and the international Anglican-Lutheran *Niagara Report.*[8] The Northern European, Canadian, and American Lutheran-Anglican agreements can be seen as regional adaptations of a single underlying vision. For all, apostolicity is a predicate first of the church and only then of ordained ministry. Continuity in apostolic mission and ministry is a complex reality with various elements and is finally grounded in the faithfulness of God to the promise to defend the Church against the gates of hell. As the *Niagara Report* states (§29): "Because the church's call to faithfulness and continuity is grounded in God's faithfulness and continuity, it is possible for the church to cherish both those symbols of continuity which the church has been given and also those experiences in its past in which God's faithfulness has persevered despite the church's brokenness, ambiguity, perversity and unfaithfulness." This more complex picture has permitted Anglicans and Lutherans a greater flexibility and openness in their attitudes toward the vexed question of ministry and unity.

An immediate question for Lutheran ecumenical discussions is whether the sort of agreements realized in Northern Europe and North America can be realized in other areas. Can other Lutheran Churches be able to develop similar agreements, most notably, the Lutheran Churches of continental Europe? These Churches face an ecumenical situation much different from either that of the Lutheran Churches of Scandinavia or that of those in North America. Nondoctrinal factors are important. But of great importance will be the perception of the relation of these Lutheran-Anglican agreements to the doctrine of justification. Can Lutherans accept episcopal succession without implying that some "human tradition or rites and ceremonies" (CA VII.3) are essential to that "true unity of the church" for which nothing is essential beyond that which is essential for justification? Differing answers to that question were at the heart of the theological side of the vehement debate over the U.S. Lutheran-Episcopal proposal. Today is not the time to rehearse those arguments, although I will note that I am firmly convinced that there is no contradiction between the recent Lutheran-Anglican agreements and a Reformation understanding of justification.

But we should ask further whether the agreement on justification reached in the *Joint Declaration* has positive implications for these ecclesiological questions. I believe the answer is "yes, but indirectly." I do not believe that any particular ecclesiology or understanding of ordained ministry is directly implied by a Reformation understanding of justification. Nevertheless, the declaration does have an impact on how Lutherans might address the ecumenical discussion of ministry and ecclesiology. Most obviously, an agreement on justification, i.e., on the heart of the Gospel, is a necessary presupposition to a reconciliation of ministries that serve that Gospel.

The more difficult question relates to the theological evaluation of ordained ministries, especially of episcopacy. The various Lutheran-Anglican agreements all affirm episcopal ministry as a sign of visible unity which, while not a guarantee, can be a significant element in the Church's continuity in apostolic mission and ministry. The understanding of justification contained in the *Joint Declaration* is not obviously in contradiction to such a valuation. (That such a valuation of episcopal ministry has been official or quasi-official in the Swedish Lutheran Church since at least the 1590s would indicate that a straightforward contradiction between such a valuation and the doctrine of justification is unlikely.) For the more exclusive, dialectical understanding of justification described above, however, a perception of contradiction is almost unavoidable. For such a view, any theological valuation of episcopal ministry is suspect; does such a valuation blur what must be kept distinct? Even if such an exclusive understanding is rejected, difficult questions about the interrelation of justification and ecclesiology remain. Some of these are explored in the 1993 international Lutheran-Catholic dialogue on *Church and Justification*. However these questions are answered, I believe the various recent Lutheran-Anglican agreements can still be affirmed. The doctrine of justification affirmed in the *Joint Declaration* makes the affirmation of the recent Lutheran-Anglican agreements easier, even if it does not dictate such an affirmation. If, as I would contend, the doctrine of justification is compatible with a variety of valuations of ordained ministry and episcopacy, then decisions about these valuations cannot be made solely on the basis of the doctrine of justification. If, in the name of upholding justification as the *sole* criterion or *the* article by which the Church stands and falls, Lutherans try to derive answers from the doctrine of justification to questions for which the doctrine of justification provides no such answer, then they will only distort the doctrine of justification, perhaps in ways that undermine the *Joint Declaration* itself.

On the international scene, Lutherans thus face the question whether agreements with Anglicans reached by the Lutheran Churches in Scandinavia and North America can be repeated in other parts of the world. The doctrine of justification and the *Joint Declaration* here play an indirect and complex role.

Even if the Lutheran-Anglican agreements on ministry can be extended to other Lutheran Churches, can they be extended to include Catholics, on the one hand, or Reformed, on the other? Can Catholics affirm the more comprehensive and flexible understanding of apostolicity and ministry which has proven acceptable to Anglicans, even to most Anglo-Catholics? In the sixteenth century, the Reformed went beyond the Lutherans in developing an alternative ecclesiology and doctrine of ministry to that of the medieval Church. Can they today affirm some form of personal, that is, individual ministry of oversight as a sign of unity and continuity? These questions do not directly relate to the topic of this essay and so I will simply state them and move on. But questions such as these now need to be taken up in Lutheran-Catholic and Lutheran-Reformed discussions.

I would, however, make a comment on the implications of both the *Joint Declaration* and the Lutheran-Anglican agreements for Lutheran-Reformed relations. As has been demonstrated in various parts of the world, when Lutherans and Reformed talk to one another about the issues that have historically divided them, they discover that these differences can be overcome. Recent events show, however, that a significant difference emerges between Lutheran and Reformed when they interact with Catholics or Anglicans. I am thinking here of the success of the revised Lutheran-Episcopal *Concordat* contrasted with the failure of Presbyterians and Episcopalians to reach agreement in the Consultation on Church Union, or of the quite different reactions of the Lutheran World Federation and the World Alliance of Reformed Churches to both the papal encyclical *Ut Unum Sint* and the jubilee indulgence proclaimed by the Vatican. The implications of this difference, not over an aspect of our relations to one another, but over our relations to a third, need to be thought through ecumenically.

III. Conclusion

The *Joint Declaration on the Doctrine of Justification*, especially when taken together with the recent extension of Lutheran-Reformed relations and the new Lutheran-Anglican agreements, changes or can change the nature of Lutheran participation in the ecumenical movement, a move-ment Lutherans were somewhat slow to join. Discussions with virtually all of the mainstream of Western Christianity can now proceed against the background of agreement on the chief article of the faith. Many dis-cussions with non-Roman Catholic Western Christians can now take place within the context of relations of full communion. The context of Lutheran ecumenical participation is thus quite different from what it was ten years ago and fundamentally different from what it was fifty years ago.

I did, however, hedge my bets. I said the *Joint Declaration* changes or can change the nature of Lutheran ecumenical participation. The decisive question now is that of reception. Reception is especially im-portant for an essentially doctrinal text, such as the *Joint Declaration*, which does not establish visible communion between the Churches and does not directly alter Church practices. The *Joint Declaration* should make us think differently, both about Lutheran-Catholic rela-tions and about the doctrine of justification itself. It is this reception into the heart and mind of the Churches that must now take place.

Notes

[1] For the most part, I have left this essay in the form in which it was delivered at the Yale Conference. I have received helpful comments on its revision from Eugene Brand.

[2] David S. Yeago, "Gnosticism, Antinomianism, and Reformation Theology: Reflec-tions on the Cost of a Construal," *Pro Ecclesia* 2 (1993) 39ff.

[3] Karl Lehmann and Wolfhart Pannenberg, eds., *The Condemnations of the Reforma-tion Era: Do They Still Divide?* trans. Margaret Kohl (Minneapolis: Fortress, 1989) 27.

[4] Karl Barth, *The Epistle to the Romans*, trans. sixth German ed., trans. Edwyn C. Hoskyns (London: Oxford University Press, 1933) 13.

[5] Günther Gassmann and Scott Hendrix, *Fortress Introduction to the Lutheran Confes-sions* (Minneapolis: Fortress Press, 1999) 173.

[6] See Bruce D. Marshall, "Faith and Reason Reconsidered: Aquinas and Luther on Deciding What Is True," *The Thomist* 63 (1999) 1–48; and Bruce D. Marshall, *Trinity and Truth*, Cambridge Studies in Christian Doctrine (Cambridge: Cambridge University Press, 1999) passim.

[7] Ephraim Radner, *The End of the Church: A Pneumatology of Christian Division in the West* (Grand Rapids, Mich.: Eerdmans, 1998) 321.

[8] *Baptism, Eucharist and Ministry*, Faith and Order Paper 111 (Geneva: World Coun-cil of Churches, 1982) and *The Niagara Report: Report of the Anglican and Lutheran Consul-tation on Episcope* (London: Anglican Consultative Council and Geneva: Lutheran World Federation, 1988.)

Chapter 6

The *Joint Declaration* and the Reformed Tradition

Gabriel Fackre

What would a *Reformed* signature on the Lutheran-Roman Catholic *Joint Declaration on the Doctrine of Justification* do for relations in Northern Ireland? Or, if consummated earlier, what would have been its effect in Puritan New England upon the arrival of immigrant Catholic folk? Or, later, for Protestant-Catholic collegiality in the South African struggle where Reformed Churches both contributed to, yet also resisted, apartheid? In the same vein, has the *Joint Declaration* had any effect so far in lands where Catholic and Lutheran populations have had a history of hostility? Or where these two traditions are now enjoined to make "this common understanding of justification . . . bear fruit in the life and teaching of the churches," and thus their mission in the world?[1] Such questions presume the sociopolitical as well as the ecclesial import of this document, its potential role in healing rifts in the wider community as well as within the Church.

To pose these kinds of questions is to reflect something of "the Reformed perspective," asked for in this consultation. Reformed Christianity is by nature *world-formative,* as Nicholas Wolterstorff has described it,[2] approaching doctrine with an eye to its worldly consequences. Thus justification is inseparable from sanctification, the latter touching society as well as souls.

But just what is "*the* Reformed perspective"? In a current volume, thirty Reformed theologians opine about the future of their tradition, giving a bewildering variety of views as to what constitutes Reformed theology.[3] From this we might wonder if there is such a thing as "the" Reformed perspective. Indeed, the greatest Reformed theologian of modern times, Karl Barth, remarked that, in spite of all our many catechisms and credos, we have "*no* Augsburg Confession, *no* Formula of Concord . . . which might later, like the Lutheran, come to possess the odor of sanctity. . . . It *may* be our doctrinal task to make a careful revision of the theology of Geneva or the Heidelberg Catechism or the Synod of Dort. . . ."[4] This commitment to reinterrogate our own tradition is illustrated by the plethora of new confessions, especially in the growing Reformed Churches of Asia and Africa.[5] If there is such diversity, does the Reformed tradition have the kind of coherence that would enable it to sign something like a "joint declaration"?

I am going to argue that the Reformed tradition does have an identity, one marked by two distinguishing characteristics, the aforementioned accent on *sanctification* with its strong social import, and a second, a focus on the divine *sovereignty*. The latter, in fact, accounts for the internal diversity within its unity. The emphasis on the glory of God, the freedom of God, means that the divine majesty forbids the domestication of deity in any human forms or formulations, that all are subject to reform. So the tradition's very name, and its battle-cry, *ecclesia reformata et semper reformanda!* As such, this second defining characteristic will prompt a second set of queries. For one, on general matters, does the *Joint Declaration* take into sufficient account that the sovereign "Lord hath more truth and light yet to break forth from his holy Word" (the words of Reformed pastor of the Pilgrims, John Robinson, as he sent the Mayflower on its way)? And on the specifics of justification, what of the aptness of Barth's concern that justification can be tied so closely to "the question of the individual experience of grace. . . . Luther's well-known question in the cloister . . . ," the "subjective appropriation of salvation," that the "objective demonstration of divine grace" by the sovereign God in the Person and Work of Christ is obscured?[6]

But turnabout is fair play. It must be asked of the Reformed: Have your two defining characteristics created their own problems—the stress on sanctification producing activist churches with little doctrinal substance, and the accent on sovereignty so distancing God from the givens—ecclesial and doctrinal—that your Churches capitulate ever and again to the Zeitgeist? These are fair questions for they discern a temptation in Reformed teaching to allow its accents to become a full-blown ideology.[7] When the Reformed *emphases* become the *sum and substance* of the Reformed tradition, rather than a *perspective on* the biblical and classical sum and substance of faith, its tradition is in crisis.

Interestingly, in a second new book on the Reformed family, ecumenist Lukas Vischer offers a counterpoint to charges of Reformed incoherence by pinpointing both its common doctrinal substance grounded in Scripture and the classical tradition, and the distinguishing perspectives identified as sanctification and sovereignty.[8]

I was made very aware of the defining marks of sovereignty and sanctification during twelve years in the recent U.S. Lutheran-Reformed dialogue. There the Lutheran *finitum capax infiniti* kept meeting the Reformed *finitum non capax infiniti*, Christ as "haveable" in Dietrich Bonhoeffer's word, the Lutheran *solidarity* of Christ *in*, *with* and *under*, encountering the Reformed *sovereignty* of Christ *over*, Christ as "unhaveable."[9] And in the second instance, the Lutheran stress on the persistence of sin in soul and society, *simul iustus et peccator*, kept confronting the Reformed *sanctificatio*, the possibility of advance in the same.[10] While these differences proved Church-dividing for centuries, when relocated in a new context of "mutual affirmation" regarding common articles of fundamental faith, they came to be understood as occasions for mutual teachability, or as it was phrased in the dialogue, "mutual admonition," eventuating in a full communion accord.

From all the foregoing it can be seen that the formula developed in that dialogue, "mutual affirmation and mutual admonition,"might prove illuminating in evaluating the *Joint Declaration*, and I shall use it in my Reformed commentary. Ecumenist Harding Meyer, commending its appearance in the U.S. Lutheran-Reformed dialogue, noted that in it "a clearly *positive function* is being attributed to the differences: the function of mutual admonition, of mutual correction, of being 'no trespassing signs.'"[11] Of course, the *Joint Declaration* and its predecessor texts are no strangers to these twins, albeit admonishments described in the language of "concerns," "emphases," and "salutary warnings."[12] Finally, differences, construed as both gifts and admonitions, have their charter in Paul's counsel to the diverse parties in the Corinthian congregation to consider each as a charism integral to the Body of Christ, but, standing alone, as an awkward substitute for the fullness of its form (1 Cor 12). Thus "the eye cannot say to the hand, 'I have no need of you. . . .'"(1 Cor 12:21).

We turn to a Reformed reading of biblical and classical understandings of justification, and then to its implications for the *Joint Declaration*.

The Centrality of Justification in the Reformed Tradition

The doctrine of justification is a fundamental teaching of the Reformed tradition. Calvin declared it to be "the principal ground on which religion must be supported," expounding it at length in his *Institutes of the Christian Religion*, with the Reformed Confessions and classical Reformed theologians following suit.[13] It has remained central in twentieth-century Lutheran-Reformed dialogues, as in the words of the North American 1983 accord, *Invitation to Action*, influenced by the 1973 European *Leuenberg Agreement*:[14]

> Both Lutheran and Reformed traditions confess [the] gospel in the language of justification by grace alone through faith alone. This doctrine was the central theological rediscovery of the Reformation; it was proclaimed by Martin Luther and by John Calvin and their respective followers.[15]

The Reformed voice on justification has been heard in some of the ecumenical dialogues with the Roman Catholic Church, as in a "common confession of faith" in the joint ecclesiological inquiry, *Towards a Common Understanding of the Church*, where Catholic and Reformed theologians were able to say together:

> Because we believe in Christ, the one Mediator between God and humankind, we believe we are justified by the grace which comes from him by means of faith which is a living and life-giving faith. We recognize that our justification is a totally gratuitous work accomplished by God in Christ.[16]

Representatives from Reformed Churches also took part in working parties that contributed to the Ecumenical Study Group whose reports concluded that the condemnations of the sixteenth century no longer apply to the present partners, and some Reformed bodies have made response to it.[17] For all that, the Yale consultation on the *Joint Declaration* is a unique venture by its inclusion of both Reformed and Anglican responses to the historic Lutheran-Catholic agreement, and is a model for larger ecumenical dialogue and witness.[18]

Yet we must deal with caveats about justification coming from some Reformed theologians who have questioned its centrality. Not *sola fide* but *soli Deo gloria* is the Reformed tradition's organizing principle, they say—not the anthropocentric questions of *our* faith or *our* works but the theocentric will and way of the sovereign God. Others have asserted that Calvin was really the "theologian of sanctification" not a theologian of justification. And recently Jürgen Moltmann has written critically about the *Joint Declaration*, holding that the justice of God in the face of the sufferings of the world is the commanding question today, not the justification of the sinner *coram Deo*.[19]

G. C. Berkouwer has demonstrated that the *sola-soli* juxtaposition is a misunderstanding of the Reformed view,[20] and Barth has rightly challenged the caricature of Calvin as only a theologian of sanctification.[21] I shall comment later on Moltmann's observation. Embedded in these judgments *are* the defining characteristics of "sovereignty" and "sanctification," but appearing as juxtaposed to justification rather than as a Reformed perspective interpreting it.

Now to the classical view of justification found in Reformed confessions and traditions and in passages from John Calvin in his *Institutes of the Christian Religion*.

Justification Encompassed: The Reformed View

In a key section of the *Institutes* Calvin develops his understanding of justification in conjunction with John 3:16: "For God so loved the world that he gave his only Son, so that everyone who believes in him may not perish but have eternal life." His use and exposition of this verse is significant because it presses justification back to its origins in the being and actions of the triune God as they address the fundamental challenge of the world's fall. As such, it reflects the characteristic Reformed accent on the divine sovereignty. Justification is conceived in macrocosmic as well as microcosmic terms. I shall call this justification *writ large*, the "objective" trinitarian and christological foundations of justification *writ small*, its "subjective" reception by faith.[22]

Driving justification back to its source in the sovereign will and way of God explains why "election" has been a constant in the Reformed tradition. Indeed, the discussion of justification in the *Institutes*, the traditional Reformed confessions and classic Reformed theologians, is set in the context of predestination, an expression of the Reformed focus on the divine sovereignty. Given both the contributions and the pitfalls of this latter preoccupation, we shall return to it as an occasion for some "mutual admonitions" between the Reformed and other Christian traditions. But my point here is that the Reformed perspective on justification, shaped by its accent on the divine sovereignty, puts to the fore the will and way of the triune God as manifest in Christ. This theocentric, rather than anthropocentric, reading is nicely illustrated by Calvin's frequent counsel on matters of election regarding the assurance of salvation, urging attention not to the state of our faith, weak and ambiguous as it always is, but to the trustworthiness of the divine deed and promise.[23] For him Jesus Christ is the "mirror" in which we look for that assurance, an assertion not unlike that of Luther's allusion to Christ as the "Book of Life" that makes for the same confidence, a theme, echoed, in fact, in the *Joint Declaration* itself.[24]

This "encompassing view" of justification might be called a *narrative* interpretation of the doctrine, as Markus Barth does in his biblical study, *Justification*.[25] Comparing it to "the liturgies of the Eastern Church and the passion plays of the Western Church," he traces it from the electing decision of God, through the Person and Work of Christ that engage the rebel world, to personal faith busy in love, and finally to the eschatological homecoming, "five days in the process of justification. . . ."[26]

In a chapter "The Beginning of Justification" Calvin takes the doctrine on its "writ large" to "writ small" journey, the grand narrative of John 3:16, albeit stated in the causal categories of his time.

> The efficient cause of our eternal salvation the Scripture uniformly proclaims to be the mercy and free love of the heavenly Father toward us; the material cause to be Christ, with the obedience by which he purchased righteousness for us; and what can be the formal or instrumental cause but faith? John includes the three in one sentence when he says, "God so loved the world, that he gave his only begotten Son, that whosoever believeth in him should not perish but have everlasting life" (John iii. 16)."[27]

He adds that Paul gathers up the three in his own formulas in both Romans and Ephesians.[28] And Calvin describes justification elsewhere in explicitly trinitarian terms: "The efficient cause of our salvation is placed in the love of the Father; the material cause in the obedience of the Son; the instrumental cause in the illumination of the Spirit, that is in faith. . . ."[29]

Calvin's wide-ranging view was carried forward in traditional Reformed teaching where the objective and subjective are brought together, as in the 1559 French Confession of Faith which declares that "on the cross we are reconciled to God and justified before him" and then "made partakers of this justification by faith alone,"[30] but done so increasingly in a decretal context, as in the distinction between "the decree of justification" and "justification . . . made in this life," yet always entailing the narrative of the electing Father, the accomplishing Son, and the *applicatio salutis* by the work of the Holy Spirit.[31]

For all the Reformed Scholasticism that pressed justification in a supralapsarian direction with its elect "us" and reprobate "them," another Reformed theologian was to come along who gave the same priority to election, and even double predestination, but took these things in quite a different direction. Thus Karl Barth speaks of a divine decision and action into which the whole of the human race is gathered up in the judgment rendered on the cross, the verdict in Jesus Christ by which man is justified. "This justifying sentence of God is His decision in which man's being as the subject of that act [of human pride] is repudiated, his responsibility for that act, his guilt is pardoned, canceled and removed." . . . "Justification definitely means the sentence executed and revealed in Jesus Christ and His death and resurrection, the No and Yes with which God vindicates Himself in relation to covenant-breaking man."[32]

True to the Reformed stress on the divine sovereignty, this verdict is rendered certainly on behalf of man, but primarily for His [God's] own sake, to assert His honor and to maintain His glory against him.[33]

The worthy stress on the *objective* dimension of justification found in the both traditional Calvinist and contemporary Barthian views does have its downside. It can become so dominant that it threatens the importance of the *subjective*, issuing in the former in a hyper-Calvinist double predestination in which the significance of the decision of faith erodes, or in the latter in which justifying faith becomes the knowledge given to some of the justification of all, rather than the graced medium through which the baptized believer is justified before God. We shall return to this later when considering the admonitions the Reformed need to hear from others. For now, let it be noted that the defining characteristic of Reformed teaching on justification is to place the microcosmic "for me" against the background of the macrocosmic "for the world." Justification in the Reformed tradition begins in the sovereign purposes of the Father, is accomplished in the saving Person and Work of the Son, and is brought through the Church to persons by the Holy Spirit's gift of faith and its sanctifying consequences. The *Leuenberg Agreement* on justification sets forth this wide-ranging view:

> The true understanding of the gospel was expressed by the fathers of the Reformation in the doctrine of justification. In this message, Jesus Christ is acknowledged as the one in whom God became [human] and bound

himself to [humanity]; as the crucified and risen one who took God's judgment upon himself and in so doing demonstrated God's love to sinners. . . . Through his word, God by His Holy Spirit calls all . . . to repent and believe, and assures the believing sinner of his righteousness in Jesus Christ. Whoever puts his trust in the gospel is justified in God's sight for the sake of Jesus Christ and is set free from the accusation of the law. In daily repentance and renewal he lives within the fellowship in praise of God and in the service of others. . . .[34]

In passing, it is worth noting that the Reformed impulse found here to treat doctrine "holistically" recurs in other loci. For example, Calvin's understanding of the Atonement, while centering on the cross, relates this priestly ministry of vicarious suffering and death to the prophetic ministry of life and teachings and royal ministry of victory announced and affected in the resurrection, as in his well-known formulation of the *munus triplex*.[35] R. S. Franks argues that this encompassing understanding of the Atonement is a major contribution of the Reformed tradition to the history of Christian thought.[36]

Affirmations

Justification in Its Fullness

We took note of how in the *Institutes* John 3:16 is the New Testament platform for a narrative view of justification. Interestingly, the *Joint Declaration (JD)* places that *same* text at the head of its paragraphs of biblical documentation. But more significantly, it treats the doctrine in the encompassing framework implied by this text, paralleling Calvin's own interpretation. The key initial statement of "The Common Understanding of Justification," echoing in places the language of John 3:16, sets forth this long and deep view of the doctrine:

> In faith we together hold the conviction that justification is the work of the triune God. The Father sent his Son into the world to save sinners. The foundation and presupposition of justification is the incarnation, death and resurrection of Christ. Justification thus means that Christ himself is our righteousness, in which we share through the Holy Spirit in accord with the will of the Father. Together we confess: by grace alone, in faith in Christ's saving work and not because of any merit on our part, we are accepted by God and receive the Holy Spirit, who renews our hearts while equipping and calling us to good works.[37]

This is a construal of the doctrine as justification writ *both* large and small, very similar to classical and current Reformed understandings. Its narrative begins with the trinitarian-christological "foundation and presupposition," the "work of the triune God" as the mercy-filled mission of the Father in sending the Son whose "incarnation, death and resurrection" overcame the world's rebellion and brought reconciliation, and moves to the work of the Holy Spirit making it available to us by grace in a faith that both "equips and calls . . . to good works."

Justification Writ Large: A "Meta-Principle" and Criterion?

Our discernment here of the difference between the "large" and "small" aspects of justification and their interrelations, may shed light on what has been described in the U.S. dialogue variously as justification as the "metalinguistic," "metatheological," or "metamethodological" principle necessary to "judge all theological formulations . . . or all theologies."[38] It also has implications for the assertion of justification as "an indispensable criterion, which constantly serves to orient all the teaching and practice of our churches to Christ" (3/18). And, possibly, for the reference to the Catholic commitment to "several criteria."

Through these Reformed spectacles, it appears that both the metaprinciple and the indispensable criterion have to do with "justification writ large." The redemption of the world by the triune God, the justification of the godless, is by grace alone, not by any human work. The "trust" that this is so has to do with "redemption accomplished" in Christ by the triune God, a norm by which all other claims to ultimacy must be measured. Touching the question of *why* the world is saved from sin, evil, and death, and *who* does it, there is one answer only: out of the love of the Father and in the deed of the Son, a divine purpose and action which alone warrants our faith, and a disavowal of trust in any other way of salvation.

If this reading is correct, the parallel of the heart of this to the 1934 Barmen Declaration is striking, as in the latter's key sentence: "Jesus Christ, as he is attested for us in Holy Scripture is the one Word of God which we have to hear and which we have to trust and obey in life and in death." Indeed, the *Joint Declaration* without the language of "criterion" says something very close to Barmen: "Lutherans and Catholics share the goal of confessing Christ, who is to be trusted above all things as the one Mediator (1 Timothy 2:5-6). . . ."[39] This Christocentricity, rooted in the Trinity, is a criteriological commitment in the face of claims to another Word, another Mediator, and thus a determinative "focus"(George Tavard) of any joint understanding of justification, and in that sense a standard for all theological formulations and proposals. All this sounds, functionally if not formally, very much like "the article by which the Church stands or falls." The conclusions of both the U.S. and European dialogues give further confirmation to its normative role. Noting the "new insights" that make today's convergences possible, the German dialogue cites and interprets the U.S. dialogue:

> [T]he barricades can be torn down only if we remain unswervingly on the Christological foundation expressed—with particular reference to the doctrine of justification—in the Lutheran-Catholic dialogue that took place in the United States: "Christ and his gospel are the source, center and norm of Christian life, individual and corporate, in church and world. Christians have no other basis for eternal life and hope of final salvation than God's free gift in Jesus Christ, extended to them in the Holy Spirit."[40]

Given the christological focus of these remarks, this assertion of Barth's is interesting:

> The *articulus stantis et cadentis ecclesiae* is not the doctrine of justification as such, but its basis and culmination: the confession of Jesus Christ in whom are hid all the treasures of wisdom and knowledge (Col 2:3); the knowledge of His being and activity for us and to us and with us. It could probably be shown that this was also the opinion of Luther . . . Christ . . . the centre, the starting point and the finishing point. . . .[41]

There is an echo here of the First Helvetic Confession of 1536 which declares that "the most sublime and principal article and the one that should be expressly set forth in every sermon . . . should be that we are preserved and saved solely by the mercy of God and the merit of Christ."[42] Indeed, it's interesting that "Luther expressed his warm approval" of this Reformed Confession.[43]

For Barth, Jesus Christ occupies that privileged place, as in the Barmen Declaration he helped to draft. Yet "Christ" as the "one Word of God" who calls us to trust and obey is inseparable from the triune God and thus bespeaks "justification writ large."

Do Barth's reservations about what constitutes the article by which the Church stands or falls shed some light on the Roman Catholic reluctance to make justification by faith the *sole* criterion for orienting all teaching and practice? Pannenberg, a not infrequent critic of Barth, appears to be open also to other criteria. He suggests that "the unity in substance of the Son with the Father . . . in a way similar to the doctrine of justification, orients the whole teaching and *praxis* of the Church . . ." might be what the Roman Catholic caveat legitimately had in mind.[44] But the trinitarian-christological grounding of justification cited in the *JD*—and in Barth's own Christocentricity—presumes just that unity. Thus justification writ large, so understood, appears to be indispensable and unique as a standard for orienting all teaching and practice, for all parties concerned.

Yet surely there is another reservation Roman Catholics have about asserting justification as the sole criterion. Walter Kasper, Carl Peter, and Avery Dulles in their comments all press a question yet to be fully addressed in ecumenical dialogue: the place of the Church vis-à-vis justification.[45] Does this reservation indicate that there is another *question* to be faced along with the one addressed by justification? Not *why* and *by* whom the reconciling work is done, but *how* the faith that receives the decision and deed of the triune God is mediated to us?

Walter Kasper's suggestion is intriguing: the way through may be to learn from the Eastern Church's stress on pneumatology, its insight that "the church does not control salvation, but it can and must pray with authority for the Spirit of Jesus Christ who mediates salvation, and it can be certain this prayer is heard on the basis of the promise made by Jesus Christ."[46] Intriguing especially for Reformed ears, for as Paul Fries has argued, "the Reformed ethos is to be explained not through its Christology as such, but through its unique conjoining of the doctrines of Christ and the Spirit."[47] The Reformed stress on the place of the Holy Spirit is directly related to its defining characteristic of *sovereignty*. A gracious divine majesty requires the work of the Holy Spirit to bring its benefits to us. As Fries says about Reformed teaching,

> The Spirit is the divine intermediary between the ascended Christ and the Christian community, working not only in the hearts of the faithful, but also through the offices and orders of the church. The real presence of the flesh and blood of Christ in the Lord's Supper is the work of the Spirit, but so is the discipline exercised by the elder.[48]

Pneumatology gives the Reformed tradition its churchly character, as reflected in its stress on discipline, orders, and offices, on the one hand, and its sacramental teaching, on the other.[49] Reformed ecclesiology has tended to stress one or the other of these, in the first case putting to the fore a view of the Church as the "visible saints" as in its congregational expressions, or in the second an "evangelical catholic" view as in its Mercersburg theology.[50] In both cases, the Holy Spirit brings Christ to us through the visible Church. If there is an article by which the Church stands or falls, such must presuppose an article on the Church itself that comes under the justification criterion. Of course, because Christ is Lord of the Church, its givens are always accountable to him as the one Word the Church always must trust and obey.

Whether it be Barth's assertion of that one Word as the higher article, or the Reformed stress on the Church of the Holy Spirit, there is a readiness here to probe further the meaning of "other criteria." Surely, "the mercy of God and the merit of Christ"—justification writ large—qualifies as a "most sublime article"(First Helvetic Confession). And its trinitarian premise cannot be without an article on the holy Catholic Church that stands or falls by the justifying Word: no head without the Body, no Son of the Father without the Holy Spirit.

Justification Writ Small

How do we get from justification writ large to the same writ small . . . to the *pro me* aspect of justification? The *JD* answers in various ways, but with a common refrain:

> By grace alone, in faith in Christ's saving work . . . we are accepted by God and receive the Holy Spirit who renews our hearts while equipping and calling us to good works (3/15); through Christ alone when we receive this salvation in faith . . . God's gift through the Holy Spirit who works through Word and Sacrament . . . and who leads believers into the renewal of life . . . . (3/16); When persons come by faith to share in Christ, God no longer imputes to them their sin and through the Holy Spirit effects in them an active love (4.2/22); We confess together that sinners are justified by faith in the saving act of God in Christ. . . . They place their trust in God's gracious promise by justifying faith, which includes hope in God and love for him (4.3/25).

In carefully worded sentences it moves narratively from "God's gracious promise" and "Christ's saving work" to the Holy Spirit's gift of faith and the renewal of life. What is said here *together* is: (1) "justifying faith" is "trust" in the "promise"; (2) this faith that justifies cannot be what it is without "hope" and "love," or, otherwise stated, without genuine "renewal" and thus "the equipping and calling to good works"; (3) throughout, all is by grace alone, excluding any human merit. Whatever other questions are involved—the naming of sin ruled by grace, the language and location of merit, the assurance of salvation—a consensus is asserted on these three points of subjective soteriology.

To these affirmations, there can only be a joyful Reformed "Amen." Here is an "inclusive" understanding of justification received. Justifying faith is the receptor of Christ's saving work, but as such is what it is only if that faith is busy in love. Justification is distinct from, but also inseparable from, sanctification (4.2/22), language identical to Calvin's and that of the Westminster Larger Catechism.[51] Conjoined are the "declaration of forgiveness" and "the renewal of life," or in Reformed lingo "regeneration." And like the Reformed accent on the divine sovereignty, grace is all the way down from justification's "beginning" to its ending, as "all persons depend completely on the saving grace of God for their salvation"(4.1/19).

Yes, an agreement on three basics, but . . . . And it is a big "but." The European dialogue, after making all the contextual, historical, and biblical qualifications that soften the sixteenth-century polarization, declares that there is "evidently a clear difference."[52] It has to do with how the saving work of Christ is applied—by imputation or impartation, by forensic declaration or by "a 'quality' intrinsically 'adhering' to the soul."[53] And from this difference follows all the related divergences on concupiscence and the *simul*, merit, the place of works, Law and Gospel.

What is at the root of this difference? Here are some Reformed speculations. Is it because for Luther, justification was a question of how the self, coming before God only with its incurved soul, must depend for salvation on Christ alone and grace alone as received by faith alone? But for the Catholic Church spread throughout the world with its corporate sense of responsibility for that realm, was it, and is it, a question how the baptized live out their faith so it might shape that world? Hence its insistence that Christ alone and grace alone empower faith to respond to that mandate? Given their concerns and even their locations, one kind of question faces "up," the other "out"? One accents pardon and the other power? One imputation, the other impartation? One *coram Deo*, the other *coram mundo*? One gravitates to Paul and the other to James? And in a Body with all its parts, how can there not be a charism to steward each kind of question and each answer? When fear descends that one's own body part could be amputated, a "salutary warning" is given. And with it also imperial claims may be made that assault other body parts.

The condemnations of the sixteenth century based on this difference, and in the hour's polemics, that were inclined to assert one's charism as definitive, are, by the October signing, now deemed inapplicable to the present partners. Why so? Is it because of fresh insights from biblical and historical studies, and theological clarification of ambiguities and misrepresentations? Surely these are important. But my Reformed spectacles discern another possible factor. The differences are livable, and even mutually teachable, now because the focus has shifted to the trinitarian-christological dimension of justification. This sounds like the conclusion in the U.S. dialogue, italicized there for emphasis:

> *Our hope of justification and salvation rests in Christ Jesus and on the gospel whereby the good news of God's merciful action in Christ is made known; we do not place our ultimate trust in anything other than God's promise and saving work in Christ.*[54]

The statement goes on to acknowledge remaining differences on justification by faith but questions whether they need be Church-dividing given the mandate to "proclaim together the one, undivided gospel of God's saving mercy in Jesus Christ."[55]

It appears here and in the *JD* that "faith" and "trust" are used in two different ways. When reference is made to "justification and salvation" writ large, we have to do with a *corporate* faith *that* "God's promise and saving work in Christ" are true. Justification writ small entails a saving *personal* faith *in* Christ. The former is juxtaposed to the belief that the world is saved by its own works. The latter stands against the belief that the self can be justified before God by its own works. In the latter are entailed Roman Catholic-Reformation differences on the relation of forensic and infused righteousness. But their tolerability, and perhaps even their mutual teachability, are made possible by a stated ultimate trust in "the one, undivided gospel of God's saving mercy in Jesus Christ."

In a time in which Jesus Christ, the Mediator, this "one Word we have to trust and obey," must be boldly declared, divided Christians find each other so they might speak it with one voice and live it out together.[56] I believe the "joint declaration" of that trinitarian-christological root of justification made it possible to view the differences on justification writ small in a new light. It created an atmosphere in which each partner can be open to the charism of other. Such agreement also enables us to see that in the polemics of the past, each was right in what it affirmed and wrong in what its extreme formulations denied. Yet the mutual condemnations continue to carry with them "concerns" and "salutary warnings" about reductionist temptations. Hence the "no trespassing signs," the readiness to receive and willingness to give admonitions. What then of a Reformed giving *and* receiving of them?

Admonitions

To Roman Catholic and Lutheran Together

The Theocentric and Anthropocentric

If the achievement of the *JD* is related to its grounding of the doctrine in justification writ large, then this "theocentric" reading should not be obscured by an anthropocentric reductionism. That is, a sole focus on the *pro me* of justification—whether justification is received by faith alone, or by faith, hope, and love, whether by imputation or impartation—will miss the big picture of justification. Whatever criticisms we might have of Karl Barth's theology, his reinterpretation of justification did bring again to the fore its trinitarian-christological grounding, and may well even have played some background role in the new consensus.[57] Let us keep our ecumenical eyes on the ultimate source and center of justification in the sovereign freedom and mercy of God manifest in the Person and Work of Jesus Christ. In the light of its own periodic drifts into anthropocentricity, this is a Reformed self-admonition as well as one to its partners.

Baptism

A refrain in the *JD* is the linkage of justification and baptism.[58] The biblical witness and ecumenical consensus expressed in the Lima document of the World Council of Churches, *Baptism, Eucharist and Ministry*[59] is reinforced and interpreted in accord with a common Catholic and Lutheran stress on the "solidarity" of Christ with givens, in this case in the firm linkage of baptism and justification. A Reformed admonition based on its "sovereignty" accent points to the dangers of allowing this "haveability" to slide into a domestication of grace that precludes both the freedom of God and the response of faith. Yes, the promise of the divine Presence in the sacramental means of grace is trustworthy, but its efficacy is inextricable from the response of faith. Thus as *Baptism, Eucharist and Ministry* states it, "The necessity of faith for the reception of the salvation embodied and set forth in baptism is acknowledged by all churches."[60] Surely this is a further area of inquiry, one where mutual admonition is in order, for a sovereignty which separates baptism from justifying grace by an abstract doctrine of predestination or universalism on the one hand, or by an antisacramental memorialism on the other, is as reductionist as a haveability emphasis that takes grace captive in our means or excludes the place of personal faith by a too narrowed *ex opere operato* interpretation.

The Public Import of Justification

The Reformed accents on both sovereignty and sanctification press the question of the implications of any agreement on justification for public issues. Why not more about this in the *Joint Declaration*? Surely this undeveloped theme must be taken up in subsequent exploration of the agreement. Here Moltmann is right in his judgment that "we need a common doctrine of righteousness-justice-justification for the 21st century."[61]

The warrants for this are found in the view of justification writ both large and small in the document itself. As seen through Reformed eyes, the redemption of the world through the will of the Father and obedience of the Son—the trinitarian-christological justification writ large—is inseparable from *sanctification* writ large. As well as being declared forgiven by the act of God in Christ, the world has been given both the gift and the call to holiness.[62] Divine sovereignty over the public sector has been worked out in the Reformed tradition in terms of the royal office of Christ within the *munus triplex*. The victory of Christ over the powers and principalities extends his rule over the counting house and voting booth as well as the soul and the Church, calling the public world to accountability and rendering possible its transformation.[63]

The grounds for public witness lie in sanctification writ small as well as large. As the objective sanctification of the world provides the range of concern and hope, the impulse and mandate in the Christian life come from the inseparability of justification and sanctification *pro me*. The personal justification of the sinner is inseparable from a personal sanctification that issues in public witness to the rule of Christ over the political, social, and economic principalities and powers, one implemented by the Church as well as persons in the struggles for social change. Thus a Reformed reading of justification will press for its "world-formative" outworking.

To the Lutheran Tradition

Lutheran-Reformed differences emerged early in Reformation history, especially so in christological and eucharistic controversies, rooted in the respective *capax* and *non capax* accents, Lutheran "solidarity" and Reformed "sovereignty."[64] In the specifics of justification, the Reformed stress on the divine sovereignty moves naturally, via its focus on election, to "justification writ large," and in so doing challenges any Lutheran preoccupation with the *pro me*, as noted by Barth.[65] From Luther's anxiety and quest for assurance, through Lutheran pietism to modern existentialisms from Kierkegaard to Bultmann, the subjective dimension of justification has bulked large, threatening to obscure its objective trinitarian-christological foundations, ones critical to the agreement reached in the *JD*.

Sanctification, the other Reformed accent, is acknowledged as well in the Lutheran tradition. However, fears of works-righteousness and ambivalence toward, or rejection of, the third use of the law, have so surrounded it with qualifications that the stress on believer's persistence in sin (the Lutheran *simul*) can obscure the possibilities of growth in grace and counsel retreat into an apolitical "interiorization of piety." Here the Reformed tradition joins the Roman Catholic in a history of insistence on the inextricability of sanctification and justification, as well as a stress on the political mandates and possibilities of sanctification.[66] Yet, for all the kinship between Reformed stress on the regenerate life and the Catholic accent on the renewed life, serious differences continue. Hence, some Reformed admonitions to the other partner.

To the Catholic Tradition

Reformed join Lutherans in the emphasis on the radical character of the Fall. Nothing in us warrants or contributes to the sinner's salvation. Hence the shared Reformation commitment to the *sola fide*. And with it the common suspicion that a Roman Catholic theology of infused righteousness invites human capacities into an equation that has room only for the divine pardon received by faith. The stress on the empowering grace of sanctification which the Reformed tradition shares with the Roman Catholic, is located, therefore, as sequential to justification, not coterminous with it as in the latter.

The same determination to give the sovereign God, rather than ourselves, all that is due, is at work in Reformed wariness about inordinate claims for human institutions as well as persons. The Church is such an institution. While different from all others, being the Body of Christ, divine as well as human and steward of the means of saving grace, it is not the unqualified extension of the Incarnation. Further, no organ constitutes the whole Body, each being a part awaiting final wholeness and healing. Hence Reformed cautions about delimiting the promises of God to any part of the household of faith. Given its finitude and flaws, the Church on earth is always *ecclesia reformata et semper reformanda*.

A Reformation-Roman Catholic dialogue on this latter point could be facilitated by attention to Reinhold Niebuhr's political theology, appreciated as it is by Roman Catholic theologians. Shaped as he was by a combined Reformed-Lutheran lineage, Niebuhr carries this Reformation realism into the realm of social history, documenting the corruptibility of every advance, critiquing the utopian claims of movements of social change, and arguing for self-criticism within institutions of power, including the Church.[67] He makes his case for this realism on the basis not only of "special revelation" but from introspection and historical inquiry. Here the Reformed doctrine of common grace and Catholic natural theology and natural law, though different in their assessment of the depth of the Fall, are in hailing distance regarding the possibilities of universal moral reasoning.[68]

And, a final admonition, one earlier noted. The Reformed stress on the divine sovereignty reminds Catholics as well as Lutherans of the limitations of a too exclusively anthropological reading of justification, with the *pro me* preoccupation neglecting its *soli Deo gloria* source and center.

To the Reformed—from Lutherans and Roman Catholics

What happens when Reformed "sovereignty" takes charge of the doctrine of justification, rather than being a perspective on it? The answer is in the history of Reformed thought on predestination. From Calvin forward, the sound impulse to ground justification in the eternal purposes of God has been accompanied by a speculative leap into the workings of the divine mind as to who is elect and who is reprobate. Thus sovereignty cum justification eventuates in theories of double predestination, controversies as to whether such is supralapsarian, infralapsarian, or sublapsarian and the like.[69] All this with a painful history of internal disputes in which one reductionism matches another, from the Dutch Arminians forward. In the same Reformed stream appears the twentieth-century Karl Barth with his new reading of the sovereign purposes of God, Christ being both elect and reprobate, with all of humanity in the Son's humiliation and exaltation. But then comes the lingering suspicion here of a structural universalism, however disavowed.[70] In all cases a single-minded stress on the divine sovereignty seems to be at work.

The admonitory corrective from other traditions comes in various ways. Lutherans have treated election as the existential testimony of the believer to the surety of election rather than a speculative theory on the source of belief and unbelief.[71] And Catholics have been concerned to assert the call for personal responsibility. These are legitimate admonitions. They counsel us to read "predestination" as the confidence that God shall be "all and in all" without the speculative details. And to be wary of "the tendency to 'explain' the doctrine by pressing the logical implications of the divine sovereignty,"[72] erasing thereby personal responsibility. Wiser, argues Reformed theologian Paul Jewett, to assert *both* a pure electing grace *and* human responsibility, and understand that as a "paradox" that may be explored but can never be explained.[73]

And admonitions are in order as well concerning aspects of Reformed thinking on sanctification. Certainly, the Lutheran stress on the *simul* must be clearly heard, reminding the Reformed tradition of its own professed realism about continuing sin, one too often overwhelmed by its stress on growth in the sanctified life. Again, Reinhold Niebuhr made the point tellingly vis-à-vis the Reformed tradition's exuberant historical expectations and theocratic pretensions when it too quickly transferred the confidences in personal growth to the public arena. Sin persists at every stage of historical advance, sobriety about which is aware of the hubris that plagues the most "righteous" social, economic, and political causes.

While the Roman Catholic tradition also finds a large place for sanctification and growth, personal and public, its ecclesial lens discerns another dimension of holiness not limited to personal or social performance. Thus the "holy" Church of the creeds has to do with a conferred status, not an achieved one, a warning to Reformed tendencies, with their legitimate emphasis on discipline, not to reduce the Church to the morally and spiritually "pure." The Reformed tradition needs an enlargement of its concept of the Church when it limits it to the "visible saints," for holiness finally roots, as it should know from its own accent on sovereignty, not in our performances but in God's purposes.[74] Indeed, it has not been without this emphasis on the objectivity of Christ's ecclesial grace, as in the Mercersburg theology, a sacramental and liturgical movement in nineteenth- and twentieth-century Reformed Churches.[75]

Jürgen Moltmann's "remarks" on the *JD* bring together both the strengths and weaknesses of the Reformed focus on sovereignty and sanctification. While rightly urging the development of a new dimension of the doctrine for a new age (thus the characteristic Reformed stress on a contextualizing *semper reformanda* under the divine sovereignty), and pressing the justice import of justification (thus the characteristic Reformed stress on society's sanctification), his comments can be read as diminishing the personal problematic of sin, the concern of another era reflected in the medieval practice of penance, to be superceded now by the twenty-first-century problematic of justice.[76] Yet the sin in the heart of every human being is a perennial problem entailing the perennial Word of judgment and justification. Further, it is reality that will come back to haunt our efforts at social change, for sin persists in the champions of justice as well as its foes. If unacknowledged and unchecked by the checking and balancing of power, it leads to the arrogance and tyranny of the self-righteous cause and social system, as well as of the self-righteous soul.[77]

A final sobering recognition with its attendant admonition. It was Lutherans in dialogue with Roman Catholics who launched and sustained this conversation in a variety of national and international settings and finalized it in an official action, *not* the Reformed Churches, or those of the left wing of the Reformation, or the Anglican communion, or any other Protestant heir. Why were the Reformed Churches not more involved in this initiative? Did it take Churches that cared deeply about classical doctrine? Surely the Roman communion does so care. And among Reformation colleagues, Lutherans over time have been the premier stewards of historic doctrine, associated, it can be argued, with its *capax*, the "haveabilty" of Christ in the givens, in this case its confessional lore (not to be altered—no 1540 *variata* version of the 1530 Augsburg Confession!). The Reformed *incapax* demands an ever-reforming Church with its ever-updated creeds and confessions, but it also has tempted us to allow the erosion of the historic doctrinal landmarks and celebrate diversity to the exclusion of unity. So our need for admonition from Lutherans and Catholics to attend to the solidarities in conjunction with the sovereignties.

Conclusion

"We intend to stay together." So declared the first assembly of the World Council of Churches in the bright early days of twentieth-century ecumenism.[78] Is the future of that "together" now in a new phase inseparable from those who have forged their own joint declaration? If so, may the Yale consultation's invitation to other communions to bring their charisms be a portent of things to come. And could an intention to "stay together" include the use of the *Joint Declaration* as a study document for parishes in local communities, much like the post-Vatican II *Living Room Dialogues?* And out of that common study could there grow a common witness to the God whose love sent an only Son to reconcile the world? And could the new amity signaled by this agreement have an impact on old conflicts in nations as well as Churches?

Whatever giant hurdles remain before a final life together of Christ's Church on earth, the *Joint Declaration* can be a landmark in mission as well as being the step toward unity that it is. May there be a "Yes" to all the previous questions. And with it a commitment to common study, proclamation, and action, testifying that Jesus Christ is the one Word of the Father whose Holy Spirit empowers us to trust and obey in life and in death.

Notes

[1] The Lutheran World Federation and the Roman Catholic Church, *Joint Declaration on the Doctrine of Justification*, English-Language Edition (Grand Rapids, Mich.: Wm. B. Eerdmans Publishing Co., 2000) Section 5, Pars. 13, 27

[2] Nicholas Wolterstorff, *Until Justice and Peace Embrace* (Grand Rapids, Mich.: Wm. B. Eerdmans Publishing Co., 1983) 3–22.

[3] David Willis and Michael Welker, eds., *Toward the Future of Reformed Theology: Tasks, Topics, Traditions* (Grand Rapids, Mich.: Wm. B. Eerdmans Publishing Co., 1999).

[4] Karl Barth, *The Word of God and the Word of Man*, trans. Douglas Horton (Boston: The Pilgrim Press, 1928) 229, 230.

[5] Discussed and documented in the essay of Eberhard Busch, "The Closeness of the Distant: Reformed Confessions after 1945," *Toward the Future of Reformed Theology*, 512–31.

[6] Karl Barth, *Church Dogmatics*, IV/1, trans. Geoffrey Bromiley (Edinburgh: T. & T. Clark, 1956) 150, 149.

[7] Of course, a temptation that attends every tradition.

[8] Lukas Vischer, "The Reformed Tradition and Its Multiple Facets," in Jean Jacques Bauswein and Lukas Vischer, eds., *The Reformed Family Worldwide: A Survey of Reformed Churches, Theological Schools and International Organizations* (Grand Rapids, Mich.: Wm. B. Eerdmans Publishing Co., 1999). See especially, "The Reformed Heritage," 26–33.

[9] In Bonhoeffer's early critique of Karl Barth's *Incapax, Act and Being*, trans. Bernard Noble (New York: Harper and Bros., 1961) 90–91.

[10] See Keith F. Nickle and Timothy F. Lull, eds., *A Common Calling: The Witness of Our Reformation Churches in North America Today* (Minneapolis: Augsburg Fortress, 1993)

35–55, and passim. Also, Gabriel Fackre and Michael Root, *Affirmations and Admonitions* (Grand Rapids, Mich.: Wm. B. Eerdmans Publishing Co., 1998) 1–43.

[11] Harding Meyer, "A Common Calling in Relation to International Agreements," *Ecumenical Trends*, vol. 23, no. 8 (September 1994) 4/116–5/117.

[12] As in Karl Lehmann and Wolfhart Pannenberg, eds., *The Condemnations of the Reformation Era: Do They Still Divide?* trans. Margaret Kohl (Minneapolis: Augsburg Fortress, 1990) 38, 40, 52, 68–69. The *JD* cites approvingly the phrase from the foregoing—"salutary warnings"—as the continuing function of the sixteenth-century condemnations (5/43). For an attack on the idea of differences as "emphases" and "concerns," see Gerhard Forde, "What Finally to Do about the (Counter-) Reformation Condemnations," *The Lutheran Quarterly*, vol. XI (1997) 3–16.

[13] John Calvin, *Institutes of the Christian Religion*, vol. II, trans. Henry Beveridge, (Grand Rapids, Mich.: Wm. B. Eerdmans Publishing Co., 1957) Book III, Chapter XI, 1, 37. In his study of justification and the Reformed Confessions, G. C. Berkouwer observes, "A single theme plays through all three documents, The Belgic Confession, the Heidelberg Catechism, and the Canons of Dort, the theme of *sola fide*." "Justification by Faith" in *Major Themes in the Reformed Tradition*, Donald McKim, ed., (Grand Rapids, Mich.: Wm. B. Eerdmans Pub. Co, 1992) 136. See also *The Second Helvetic Confession*, XV, XVI, and Heinrich Heppe summarizing Reformed teaching in his compendium *Reformed Dogmatics*, trans. G. T. Thompson (Grand Rapids, Mich.: Baker Book House, 1978) 543: "The whole evangelical doctrine of salvation stands or falls with the doctrine of justification as being the inmost core of the doctrine of redemption."

[14] Now more than European in its ninety national Churches, including five from South America. See *Die Kirche Jesu Christi: Der reformatorische Beitrag zum ökumenischen Dialog über die kirchliche Einheit* (Frankfurt am Main: Verlag Otto Lembeck, 1995).

[15] "Joint Statement on Justification," in *Invitation to Action: The Lutheran-Reformed Dialogue Series III, 1981–1983*, James E. Andrews and Joseph A. Burgess, eds., (Philadelphia: Fortress Press, 1984) 9. A section from the *Leuenberg Agreement*, reflecting this consensus, "The Message of Justification as the Message of the Free Grace of God," was incorporated into the 1997 U.S. Lutheran-Reformed "Formula of Agreement."

[16] "Our Common Confession of Faith," *Towards a Common Understanding of the Church: Reformed/Roman Catholic International Dialogue, Second Phase* (Geneva: World Alliance of Reformed Churches, 1991) 29. Note too the commentary on it and other Roman Catholic-Reformed conversations in Martien E. Brinkman and Henk Witte, eds., *From Roots to Fruits: Protestants and Catholics Toward a Common Understanding of the Church* (Geneva: World Alliance of Reformed Churches, 1998).

[17] *The Condemnations of the Reformation Era: Do They Still Divide?* alludes to that participation. The Arnoldshain Conference in Germany that includes Reformed Churches made a response to the *Joint Declaration*.

[18] A regional New England consultation modeled on this one, cooperatively planned by Roman Catholic, Lutheran, Reformed, and Episcopal ecumenists took place on April 10, 2000, in Acton, Massachusetts.

[19] "*Bemerkungen zur 'Gemeinsamen Erklärung zur Rechtfertigungslehre' (GER) und zur 'Gemeinsamen offiziellen Feststellung'(GOF)*."

[20] See the discussion and rejection of this in G. C. Berkouwer, "Justification by Faith," in *Major Themes in the Reformed Tradition*, Donald McKim, ed., 140–41.

[21] So Barth's observation and refutation in *Church Dogmatics*, IV/2, trans. G. W. Bromiley (Edinburgh: T. & T. Clark, 1958) 509–10. Interestingly, he earlier assigned the contributions of Calvin to the royal office of sanctification and Luther to the priestly office of justification. *Church Dogmatics* IV/1, 145–46.

[22] As in John Murray, *Redemption Accomplished and Applied* (Grand Rapids, Mich.: Wm. B. Eerdmans Publishing Co., 1980).

[23] John Hesselink traces such out in Calvin's catechism, and throughout the *Institutes*. See I. John Hesselink, *Calvin's First Catechism: A Commentary* (Louisville: Westminster/John Knox, 1997) 96–98.

[24] Calvin, *Institutes of the Christian Religion*, Vol. II, Book III, Chapter XXIV, par. 5, 244. See the reference to the Book of Life in *The Formula of Concord*, Art. 11, Sect. 2. And in the *JD* all the paragraphs on assurance in 4.6, 34–36.

[25] Markus Barth, *Justification: Pauline Texts Interpreted in the Light of Old and New Testaments* (Grand Rapids, Mich.: Wm. B. Eerdmans Publishing Co., 1971).

[26] Ibid., 21.

[27] John Calvin, *Institutes of the Christian Religion*, Vol. II, Book III, Chapter XIV, par. 17, 85. He includes a fourth, citing Paul, a "final cause" being the demonstration of the divine righteousness.

[28] Ibid., 86–87.

[29] Ibid., 88. See also Vol. II, Book II, Chapter XVII, where John 3:16 is exegeted and causal language deployed.

[30] "The French Confession of Faith, 1559," XVII, XX, in Arthur C. Cochrane, ed., *Reformed Confessions of the 16th Century* (Philadelphia: Westminster Press, 1966) 150, 151.

[31] See Heppe, *Reformed Dogmatics*, 557 and passim.

[32] Barth, *Church Dogmatics*, IV/1, 145, 96. See also how Eberhard Jüngel has incorporated this aspect into his reading of justification, a factor that may have contributed to his initial questioning and later endorsement of the *Joint Declaration*. Eberhard Jüngel, "On the Doctrine of Justification," *International Journal of Systematic Theology* (1999), vol. 1, no.1, 25: "The centre of Christian proclamation is that the history of Jesus Christ is not a private affair, but that, in that history, God's history with the whole of humanity takes place, and that in this one, unique history there occurs a liberating change of direction in the deadly fate of sin-dominated humanity. . . ." See also his "Kardinale Probleme," *Stimmen Der Zeit*, *Heft* 11 (November 1999) 727–35.

[33] *Church Dogmatics*, IV/1, 98.

[34] "The Message of Justification as the Message of the Free Grace of God," *Leuenberg Agreement* II/6/1 in *Invitation to Action*, Andrews and Burgess, eds., 67.

[35] Calvin, *Institutes of the Christian Religion*, Vol. 1, Book II, Chapter XV, 425–32.

[36] Robert S. Franks, *The Work of Christ: A Historical Study of Christian Doctrine* (London: Thomas Nelson, Ltd., 1962) 333–51. Its ecumenical import can be seen in the use made of the threefold office in the Decree on the Apostolate of the Laity, *The Documents of Vatican II*, ed. Walter Abbott, s.j. (N.Y.: Guild Press, 1966) 491–95.

[37] *JD*, 3/15.

[38] So summarized by George Tavard in *Justification: An Ecumenical Study* (New York: Paulist Press, 1983) 62.

[39] *JD*, 3/18.

[40] "Justification," in *The Condemnations of the Reformation Era: Do They Still Divide?* Lehmann and Pannenberg, eds., 36. The quotation is from H. G. Anderson, T. Austin Murphy, Joseph A. Burgess, eds., *Justification by Faith: Lutherans and Catholics in Dialogue VII* (Minneapolis: Augsburg, 1985), "Common Statement," 71.

[41] *Church Dogmatics*, IV/1, 527–29.

[42] "The First Helvetic Confession of 1536," *Reformed Confessions of the 16th Century*, Cochrane, ed., 104.

[43] Ibid., 98, editor Arthur Cochrane's comment.

[44] Wolfhart Pannenberg, "New Consensuses, Defused Conflicts, Protestant Anxieties," slightly abridged translation, 1999 of article in "Idea," 2.2. 1998; reprinted in "EPD Dokumentation" 11/98.

[45] See Walter Kasper, "Basic Consensus and Church Fellowship" in Joseph Burgess, ed., *In Search of Christian Unity: Basic Consensus/Basic Difference* (Minneapolis: Augsburg

Fortress, 1991) especially 34–39; Carl Peter, "Justification by Faith and the Need of Another Critical Principle," in *Justification by Faith*, Anthony, Murphy, Burgess, eds., 304–15; Avery Dulles, "Two Languages of Salvation," *First Things*, no. 98 (December 1999) 25–30. It should be noted that the study by the Faith and Order Commission of the World Council of Churches is relevant to this deficit, *The Nature and Purpose of the Church: A Stage on the Way to a Common Statement*, Faith and Order Paper No. 181, November 1998 (Geneva: WCC/Faith and Order, 1998).

[46] Kasper, "Basic Consensus and Church Fellowship," 39.

[47] Paul Fries, "Fundamental Consensus and Church Fellowship: A Reformed Perspective,"in *In Search of Christian Unity*, Burgess, ed., 157–58.

[48] Ibid., 158.

[49] Also on the high profile it gives to Israel as visible people of the covenant. There is an extensive current Reformed literature on anti-supersessionism, the latter discussed in the writer's *The Doctrine of Revelation: A Narrative Interpretation* (Edinburgh: Edinburgh University Press, 1997 and Grand Rapids, Mich.: Wm. B. Eerdmans Publishing Co., 1997) 107–19.

[50] On the former, see Alan P. F. Sell, *Saints: Visible, Orderly and Catholic: The Congregational Idea of the Church* (Allison Park, Pa.: Pickwick Press, 1986), and on the latter the literature on the Mercersburg movement, the school of thought associated with the nineteenth-century Reformed seminary in Mercersburg, Pennsylvania, its theologians, John Williamson Nevin and Philip Schaff, and the journal, *The Mercersburg Review*. This "evangelical catholic" wing of the Reformed tradition is still alive and well through it *New Mercersburg Review* and Mercersburg Society. For some of the original writings, see Charles Yrigoyen Jr. and George H. Bricker, *Catholic and Reformed: Selected Theological Writings of John Williamson Nevin* (Pittsburgh: The Pickwick Press, 1978) and Yrigoyen and Bricker, *Reformed and Catholic: Selected Historical and Theological Writings of Philip Schaff* (Pittsburgh: The Pickwick Press, 1979).

[51] "Although sanctification be inseparably joined with justification, yet they differ, in that God in justification imputeth the righteousness of Christ; in sanctification, his Spirit infuseth grace, and enableth to the exercise thereof; in the former sin is pardoned; in the other, it is subdued . . . " *Westminister Larger Catechism*, Q. 77.

[52] Lehmann and Pannenberg, *The Condemnations of the Reformation Era: Do They Still Divide?* 47.

[53] Ibid.

[54] "Common Statement, Introduction," *Justification by Faith*, Anthony, Murphy, Burgess, eds., 16.

[55] Ibid.

[56] A conclusion to which Avery Dulles seems to come, after raising questions about how much reconciliation of views was in fact achieved by the *JD*, "Two Languages of Salvation: The Lutheran-Catholic Joint Declaration," 29–30.

[57] The possibility of this is suggested by Barth's commendation of Hans Küng's study, *Justification: The Doctrine of Karl Barth and a Catholic Reflection*, trans. Thomas Collins, Edmund E. Tolk and David Granskou, with a letter by Karl Barth (New York: Thomas Nelson, 1964) xix–xxii. However, there is a misreading of Barth by Küng traced in detail by Alister McGrath in "Justification: Barth, Trent and Küng," *The Scottish Journal of Theology* 34 (1981) 517–29. Nevertheless, Küng's discernment of the "objective" dimension in Barth as "the primary and decisive aspect of the theology of justification"(72) is correct and the point at hand. See also Eberhard Busch's essay written against the background of the current discussion of the *JD*. "Karl Barth's Doctrine of Justification,"typescript, 1999.

[58] *JD*, 4.4, 28–30.

[59] As in "The Meaning of Baptism," *Baptism, Eucharist and Ministry*, Faith and Order Paper 111 (Geneva: World Council of Churches, 1982) 2–4.

[60] *Baptism, Eucharist and Ministry*, 3.

[61] Moltmann, "*Bemerkungen zur 'Gemeinsamen Erklärung zur Rechtfertigungslehre' (Ger) und zur 'Gemeinsamen offiziellen Feststellung' (GOF)*, 2.

[62] Developed by Barth in *Church Dogmatics*, IV/2 as the exaltation of the Son, and the transformation of the world *de iure.*

[63] A theme explored by W. A. Visser t'Hooft in *The Kingship of Christ* (New York: Harper & Brothers, 1948) and expressed with power during World War II by Karl Barth in his *Letter to Great Britain from Switzerland* (London: The Sheldon Press, 1941) 9–11ff.

[64] See *Affirmations and Admonitions, op. cit.*, 1–43, and Gabriel Fackre, "What the Lutherans and Reformed Can Learn from One Another," *The Christian Century*, vol. 114, no. 18 (June 4–11, 1997) 558–61.

[65] *Church Dogmatics*, IV/1, 150.

[66] Indeed, Calvin uses the language of "reward" alluded to in the *JD*'s "Catholic understanding" of good works, declaring that "the faithful are rewarded with the promises which God gave in his law to the cultivators of righteousness and holiness," surrounding it, however with the "threefold" qualification that works have nothing to do with justification which comes by faith alone, they are God's own gift being so honored, and their manifest pollutions are pardoned. (Calvin, *Institutes of the Christian Religion*, Vol II, Book III, Chapter XVII, par. 3, 106.)

[67] See Reinhold Niebuhr, *The Nature and Destiny of Man*, vols. 1 and 2 (New York: Charles Scribner's Sons, 1968) passim, and the writer's *The Promise of Reinhold Niebuhr* (Lanham, Md.: University Press of America, 1994).

[68] The role of common grace and the "covenant with Noah"—general revelation—vis-à-vis special revelation is discussed in Fries' *The Doctrine of Revelation*, 37–178.

[69] For a comparison of the three, see Paul K. Jewett, *Election and Predestination* (Grand Rapids, Mich.: Wm. B. Eerdmans Publishing Co., 1985) 83–105.

[70] On the disavowal, see Karl Barth, *Church Dogmatics*, IV/3/1, trans. G. W. Bromiley, (Edinburgh: T. and T. Clark, 1961) 477–78.

[71] See this observation in the North American Lutheran-Reformed dialogue: Meyer, "A Common Calling," 54–55.

[72] Jewett, *Election and Predestination*, 78.

[73] Ibid., 92, 106–09, 113–14, 136–39. See Also Donald Baillie on "the paradox of grace," in *God Was in Christ: An Essay on Incarnation and Atonement* (New York: Charles Scribner's Sons, 1948) 114–18. So too Jonathan Edwards on "efficacious grace" in "Miscellaneous Remarks," *Works*, vol. VII, iv, 48.

[74] Ironically, here the Reformed tradition's own teaching of the divine sovereignty, muted in this case by its zealous partner, sanctification.

[75] See the earlier references to Nevin and Schaff.

[76] The industrial missioner Horst Symanowski anticipated this point in the heyday of the secular theologies of the 1960s in oft-repeated words: In the sixteenth century, Luther lay awake at night asking, "How can I find a gracious God?" Today we lie awake asking, "How can we find a gracious neighbor?" Thus yesterday the problem was the alienation between the soul and God. Today it is the estrangement between black and white, rich and poor, East and West, men and women, young and old.

[77] An uncritical naivete about the corruptibility of the righteous cause to which my own Reformed tradition is regularly tempted, as acknowledged in Fackre, "What Lutherans and Reformed Have to Learn from Each Other," 558–61.

[78] The writer as a student was present at the 1948 Amsterdam Assembly, hearing this earlier "joint declaration" read on its final day.

Chapter 7

The *Joint Declaration* on the Doctrine of Justification: A Significant Ecumenical Achievement

Edward Idris Cassidy

I. Introduction

The consensus document, known as the *Joint Declaration on the Doctrine of Justification*, must surely be considered to be one of the most important acquisitions of the modern ecumenical movement.

While this document involves directly only the Lutheran World Federation and the Roman Catholic Church, other members of the Christian family cannot ignore it. For all the reformers, the doctrine of justification was seen as the article of faith on which the Church stands or falls. They considered justification by faith to be a criterion or corrective for all Church practices, structure, and theology. It was to be understood as being at the heart of the Gospel's proclamation of God's free and merciful promises in Jesus Christ that can rightly be received only through faith.

In fact, the doctrine of justification has been dealt with in the theological dialogue between the Roman Catholic Church and the World Alliance of Reformed Churches, as well as in the Anglican-Roman Catholic International Commission. But nowhere else have the results of dialogue on this subject been submitted for formal, official reception, as in the present case. At the executive committee meeting of the World Methodist Council in Hong Kong in September 1999, it was agreed that the officers of the council would send a letter of congratulations to the Lutheran World Federation (LWF) and the Pontifical Council for Promoting Christian Unity (PCPCU) over the *Joint Declaration*. The Methodists saw themselves as inheriting indirectly the

Lutheran view of justification and expressed the belief that the *Joint Declaration* would change the ecumenical scene for all Christians.

From the beginning of the formal Lutheran-Roman Catholic theological dialogue, the doctrine of justification has been an important topic. A special committee of the Roman Catholic-Lutheran dialogue commission which formulated the *Joint Declaration*, had at its service the earlier dialogue reports prepared by the commission. To understand fully the consensus reached in the *Joint Declaration*, it is necessary to consider this document together with those earlier reports, especially the 1972 report of the Joint Lutheran/Roman Catholic study commission *The Gospel and the Church* (Malta Report) and the 1994 report of the same commission, entitled *Church and Justification.*[1] Two other dialogue documents of special importance in this process leading to consensus were *Justification by Faith* from the USA Roman Catholic/Lutheran dialogue in 1983 and the study of an ecumenical working group of Protestant and Catholic theologians in Germany that published its findings in 1986 in a volume entitled, *The Condemnations of the Reformation Era: Do They Still Divide?*[2]

While we stress the importance of the *Joint Declaration*, and joyfully celebrate its official reception by the two Churches, we need to keep in mind also its precise nature and limitations.

The *Joint Declaration* is not a new confessional statement, nor is it a compromise document. It seeks to summarize the results of the Lutheran/Roman Catholic dialogue on this doctrine over a period of some thirty years by stating what each community holds as its faith in basic truths of this doctrine and showing that the two explications of these basic truths are not contrary one to the other.

I believe this is an important aspect of the *Joint Declaration*. A fundamental principle in ecumenical dialogue is that there may be a distinction between the doctrines of faith and the manner in which these doctrines are formulated or expressed. Pope John XXIII stated this already at the opening of the Second Vatican Council, and it finds an important place in the *Ecumenical Directory of the Holy See*, published in 1993. This means that the same truth may be expressed in different traditions in diverse forms, without that necessarily implying diversity in faith. Of course, the theological dialogue, and then the Churches concerned, have to discern when this is the case. Diversity of expression may enrich faith understanding. It may also, however, wound unity and divide Christians.

The *Joint Declaration* can, I believe, make another important contribution to the ecumenical movement and to the life of the Lutheran and

Catholic communities. In an article published in the February number of the Catholic publication *30 Giorni*, Professor Harding Meyer expresses the conviction that, since the mid-sixties of the last century, there has been a tendency in all the Churches to promote what he calls "an action oriented model of faith," completely centered on the *praxis pietatis*. Its concern is active life, especially under its social aspect. Certainly, there is this tendency in Catholic liturgy, theology, and pastoral activity to concentrate on good proposals, social action, and works of mercy. All this is of course part of the Christian witness, but a well-known Catholic preacher was able to stress the priority to be given in catechesis to the action of divine grace in the work of salvation in a sermon before the Pope and the Roman Curia by the following statement:

> I often ask myself sorrowfully why it is that, in so many parts of the world, thousands of faithful are drawn away from the Catholic Church so as to hear elsewhere the strong and liberating message that "those who are in Christ Jesus are not condemned" (Rom 8:1). Why not let this ring out loud in our preaching to the people of God?[3]

The *Joint Declaration* in paragraph 15 reminds the Churches of this priority and so makes a valuable contribution to the celebration of the jubilee year:

> Together we confess: By grace alone, in faith in Christ's saving work and not because of any merit on our part, we are accepted by God and receive the Holy Spirit, who renews our hearts while equipping and calling us to good works.

How appropriate it is that we have arrived, together with the Lutheran World Federation at this common understanding of justification which praises the work of the triune God and focuses on the saving work of Christ, precisely at the time of formal preparations for the year 2000. For these preparations following the plan of *Tertio Millennio Adveniente*, were designed to praise the triune God and were "deeply charged with Christological significance" (TMA 31). Certainly for Catholics this achievement enhances our celebration of the Great Jubilee and provides a decisive ecumenical step into this new century. As we commemorate in the year 2000 the birth of Christ, we are now able to say, in humility and with gratitude to God, that we have tried to respond to the prayer of our Lord for his disciples, "that they may all be one" (John 17:21) and that there are some tangible results that we can now offer, even though we realize that we still have a long way to go towards the goal of visible unity to which Christ calls us.

We must not, of course, expect the *Joint Declaration* to indicate that a consensus has been reached between Catholics and Lutherans on all aspects of the doctrine of justification. Nor does it attempt to cover other doctrinal questions, such as the sacraments, ministry, Eucharist, and authority, that are still subjects for study by the Joint International Lutheran/Roman Catholic Commission for Unity. The document states clearly that the consensus reached refers to "basic truths concerning the doctrine of justification and that the remaining differences in its explication are no longer the occasion for doctrinal condemnation" (cf. Art. 5).

Of particular interest to the whole ecumenical movement is, I believe, the reception process that led to the signing in Augsburg, Germany, of the *Joint Declaration*, on 31 October 1999.

In February 1997 the *Joint Declaration on the Doctrine of Justification* was formally submitted to the Lutheran World Federation and to the Holy See for study and an official response. In each case the process was different, due to the different understanding of each of the partners as to where authority is found that can give such approval.

In the course of the following year, member Churches of the Lutheran World Federation examined the document in their synods, and on 16 June 1998 the LWF Council was able to declare that an almost unanimous response from the synods had been in favor of accepting the declaration. The council therefore approved unanimously the *Joint Declaration*. This was the first time that the Lutheran World Federation had ever attempted such a process, and I believe it can be said that in so doing, the LWF established a new milestone in its own self-understanding as a communion of Churches.

The process of reception within the Catholic Church was quite different. A number of local churches had been consulted on the earlier versions of the *Joint Declaration*, but now the final approval was entrusted to the Pontifical Council for Promoting Christian Unity in close consultation with the Congregation for the Doctrine of the Faith. After much study, consultation, and discussion, the Pontifical Council for Promoting Christian Unity was able to announce on 25 June 1998, that "a consensus had indeed been reached in basic truths of the doctrine of justification."

At the same time, our response indicated several points that seemed to us to require further study and clarification. Something similar had happened also within the Council of the Lutheran World Federation, which had noted some aspects of the document that troubled member Churches.

The Vatican response, however, was the cause of considerable disquiet on the part of the Lutheran World Federation, which doubted seriously that both parties were in fact in full agreement about what they were signing, were the *Joint Declaration* to be signed in such circumstances.

In the months that followed, the Pontifical Council for Promoting Christian Unity sought in various ways to explain more clearly the positive nature of its official response, but it became clear that something more was required. The two parties therefore sought to prepare a short explanatory document that would affirm the positive statement made by the Holy See, while at the same time seeking to clarify further those points which had been indicated by both parties as requiring more study.

These efforts proved successful and resulted in an *Official Common Statement* that was signed together with the *Joint Declaration*, and to which is attached an *Annex*. These new documents duly received the approval of the LWF Council and the Holy See, and as I have already mentioned, on 31 October 1999, in Augsburg, Germany, a formal signing took place in a ceremony that will be long remembered by those who were present and I believe by millions of Catholics and Lutherans throughout the world.

II. The *Joint Declaration*

The *Joint Declaration* aims to show the following:

> On the basis of their dialogue the subscribing Lutheran churches and the Roman Catholic Church are now able to articulate a common understanding of our justification by God's grace through faith in Christ [. . .]. The remaining differences in its explication are no longer the occasion for doctrinal condemnations (*JD* 5).

The document begins with a preamble (1–7), *and* then gives the main points of the biblical message of God's work of justifying fallen human beings. This is followed by an analysis of the doctrine of justification as an ecumenical problem between the Catholic Church and the Churches stemming from the Reformation. The result of recent dialogues is then stated as the present-day common, or shared understanding of justification.

The document has the following structure:

1. Biblical Message of Justification (8–12)
2. The Doctrine of Justification as Ecumenical Problem (13)

3. The Common Understanding of Justification (14–18)
4. Explicating the Common Understanding of Justification
    1. Human Powerlessness and Sin in Relation to Justification (19–21)
    2. Justification As Forgiveness of Sins and Making Righteous (22–24)
    3. Justification by Faith and through Grace (25–27)
    4. The Justified As Sinner (28–30)
    5. Law and Gospel (31–33)
    6. Assurance of Salvation (34–36)
    7. The Good Works of the Justified (37–39)
5. The Significance and the Scope of the Consensus Reached.

Without seeking to present more fully the *Joint Declaration*, I would draw your attention to the three basic truths on the doctrine of justification concerning which the Catholic Church and the Lutheran World Federation have reached a consensus. These are found in the *Joint Declaration*, in Section 3, nos. 14–18.

First, justification is a free gift bestowed by the trinitarian God and centers on the person of Christ who became incarnate, died, and rose. In being related to the person of Christ through the work of the Holy Spirit, we enter into the condition of righteousness. This is not something that we merit, but is freely bestowed. And so "together we confess: By grace alone, in faith in Christ's saving work and not because of any merit on our part, we are accepted by God and receive the Holy Spirit, who renews our hearts while equipping and calling us to good works" (no. 15). This statement is the heart of the *Joint Declaration* and is in perfect accord with both the Augsburg Confession and with the Decree on Justification of the Council of Trent. It dispels some false stereotypes inherited from the past, when Lutherans have often accused Catholics of teaching that justification is a human achievement rather than a divine gift received in faith, while Catholics have understood Lutherans as holding that justification does not involve inner renewal or require good works. By mentioning both faith and works, both acceptance by God and the gift of the Holy Spirit, this fundamental statement responds to such accusations.

Second, we receive this salvation in faith. Faith is itself God's gift through the Holy Spirit who works through word and sacrament in the community of the believers and who, at the same time, leads believers into that renewal of life that God will bring to completion in eternal life. Hence, the reality of justification is linked to faith, but not simply as an intellectual assent of the mind. Rather, the believer is to give himself or herself over to Christ in the renewal of life.

Third, justification points to the heart of the Gospel message, but must be seen in an organic unity with all the other truths of faith: Trinity, Christology, ecclesiology, and sacraments. "It stands in an essential relation to all the truths of faith, which are to be seen as internally related to each other. It is an indispensable criterion which constantly serves to orient all the teaching and practice of our Churches to Christ" (no. 18).

The common understanding of justification expressed in the *Joint Declaration* is trinitarian and Christocentric in character. The core of it, to cite the *Joint Declaration* (no. 15), is that "in faith we together hold the conviction that justification is the work of the triune God. The Father sent his Son into the world to save sinners. The foundation and the presupposition of justification is the incarnation, death, and resurrection of Christ. Justification thus means that Christ himself is our righteousness, in which we share through the Holy Spirit in accord with the will of the Father."

III. The *Official Common Statement*

As mentioned already, during the reception process of the *Joint Declaration*, an *Official Common Statement* was agreed to by both the Lutheran World Federation and the Catholic Church to make it quite clear that both parties were in fact in full agreement about the consensus that had been reached. This document was to be signed together with the *Joint Declaration* and it states as follows:

1. "On the basis of the agreements reached in the *Joint Declaration on the Doctrine of Justification*, the Lutheran World Federation and the Catholic Church declare together: 'The understanding of the doctrine of justification set forth in this *Declaration* shows that a consensus in basic truths of the doctrine of justification exists between Lutherans and Catholics' (*JD* 40). On the basis of this consensus the Lutheran World Federation and the Catholic Church declare together: 'The teaching of the Lutheran Churches presented in this *Declaration* does not fall under the condemnations of the Council of Trent. The condemnations in the Lutheran Confessions do not apply to the teaching of the Roman Catholic Church presented in this *Declaration*' (*JD* 41)."
2. Having confirmed without reservation these two fundamental statements of the *Joint Declaration*, the *Official Common Statement* explains that the questions raised by the Council of the Lutheran World Federation in

its Resolution on the *Joint Declaration*, dated June 1998, and by the Catholic Church in its response to the *Joint Declaration* on June 25 of 1998 have been dealt with in a document attached to the *Official Common Statement*. This document, under the title of *Annex*, "further substantiates the consensus reached in the *Joint Declaration*; thus it becomes clear that the earlier mutual doctrinal condemnations do not apply to the teaching of the dialogue partners as presented in the *Joint Declaration*."

3. A third paragraph of the *Official Common Statement* commits the two parties to "continued and deepened study of the biblical foundations of the doctrine of justification," and to seeking "further common understanding of the doctrine." It indicates that "[b]ased on the consensus reached, continued dialogue is required specifically on the issues mentioned in the *Joint Declaration* itself (*JD* 43) as requiring further clarification, in order to reach full church communion." And, finally, it declares that "Lutherans and Catholics will continue their efforts ecumenically in their common witness to interpret the message of justification in language relevant for humans beings today, and with reference both to individual and to social concerns of our times."

IV. The *Annex*

The official response of the Catholic Church to the *Joint Declaration* indicated three principal concerns: (a) the explications in *JD* 4.4 on The Justified As Sinner—*JD* 28–30; (b) justification as criterion for the life and practice of the Church—*JD* 18; and (c) the new life that comes to the justified from divine mercy, and with particular reference to the use of the expressions *cooperatio* and *mere passive* in *JD* 21.

No. 2 of the *Annex* recalls the basic understanding common to the two parties as expressed in *JD* 15:

> "Together we confess: By grace alone, in faith in Christ's saving work and not because of any merit on our part, we are accepted by God and receive the Holy Spirit, who renews our hearts while equipping and calling us to good works."

There follows in 2 A a more detailed explanation of the biblical teaching on the gift of new life in Christ that God imparts to his children, and states that "we are truly and inwardly renewed by the action of the Holy Spirit, remaining always dependent on his work in us." It recalls St. Paul's words to the Corinthians: "So if anyone is in Christ, there is a new creation: everything old has passed away; see, everything has become new!" (2 Cor 5:17). "The justified do not remain sinners in this sense."

The *Annex* makes clear, however, that "yet we would be wrong were we to say that we are without sin." The Sacred Scriptures and our liturgies remind us of "the persisting danger which comes from the power of sin and its action in Christians," and "to this extent, Lutherans and Catholics can together understand the Christian as *simul iustus et peccator*, despite their different approaches to this subject as expressed in *JD* 29–30."

In 2B, the *Annex* explains the different senses in which Lutherans and Catholics use the concept of "concupiscence." Does concupiscence, that is to say, our innate tendency to be self-indulgent, make us sinners, even when we do not give in to it? There seemed to be an apparent contradiction in the statement of the *JD* that "concupiscence is truly sin," and the Council of Trent which condemned under anathema the view that concupiscence is sin (DS 1515). The *Annex* seeks at some length to explain that the problem here lies with use of the same words for different understandings of the relationship of justification and disorderly desires and spiritual weakness that afflict our fallen nature, but are not judged to undermine the basic consensus reached on the doctrine of justification.

The relationship between justification which takes place "by grace alone" and "apart from works," and the new life which comes to us through the reception of God's gift of interior renewal is taken up in *Annex* 2C, 2D, and 2E. There are several references to the Lutheran Confessional writings which support the following quotation from the Book of Concord: "as soon as the Holy Spirit has initiated his work of regeneration and renewal in us through the Word and the holy sacraments, it is certain that we can and must cooperate by the power of the Holy Spirit" (FC, SD II, 64f.). And then as regards the question of reward, the Formula of Concord is again quoted to clarify any misunderstanding in this connection:

> It is God's will and express command that believers should do good works which the Holy Spirit works in them, and God is willing to be pleased with them for Christ's sake and he promises to reward them gloriously in this and in the future life (FC, SD IV, 38).

At the same time, the *Annex* concludes this section with the statement that "any reward is a reward of grace on which we have no claim."

Finally, on the question of justification as "measure or touchstone for the Christian faith," the *Annex* (no. 3) has the following clarification:

"No teaching may contradict this criterion. In this sense, the doctrine of justification is 'an indispensable criterion which constantly serves to orient all the teaching and practice of our churches to Christ' (JD 18). As such, it has its truth and specific meaning within the overall context of the church's fundamental Trinitarian confession of faith. We 'share the goal of confessing Christ in all things, who alone is to be trusted above all things as the one Mediator (1 Tim 2:5f.) through whom God in the Holy Spirit gives himself and pours out his renewing gifts' (JD 18)."

The *Official Common Statement* calls "the two partners in dialogue . . . to continued and deepened study of the biblical foundations of the doctrine of justification." Not all Lutheran or Catholic theologians have expressed complete satisfaction with the *Joint Declaration* and further dialogue may prove opportune in order to clarify and deepen even further the consensus already reached. This would seem to be especially required in regard to the relationship between justification and sanctification, and what it means to confess that justification brings about the regeneration, transformation, and divinization of the sinner.

The *Joint Declaration* itself sets before us a number of questions that await our joint attention. "These include, among other topics, the relationship between the Word of God and church doctrine, as well as ecclesiology, ecclesial authority, church unity, ministry, the sacraments, and the relation between justification and social ethics" (JD 43). The dialogue is in fact continuing. It has its stated aim, as set out in the *Official Common Statement*, no. 3, to "reach full church communion, a unity in diversity, in which remaining differences would be 'reconciled' and no longer have a divisive force." This recognition of our common goal is in itself a significant ecumenical commitment.

V. Pastoral Consequences

A first consequence of the signing of this *Joint Declaration* is the realization that we have been able to overcome one of the fundamental differences that has distinguished us as two communities. This should have a positive and real effect not only on the future theological dialogue, but also on our communities at every level. We should now be able to appreciate more all that binds us together as sons and daughters of the one Lord, to whom we look to as the one Mediator between God and his people. Serious difficulties remain, but they are secondary to what we hold in common. No longer may we look upon our different expressions of faith as being two huge canons drawn up in battle line and facing each other!

Secondly, we must now be deeply aware of the need to move further along the path to unity. We have not reached the end of the road. We have certainly made good progress and opened the way to further achievements. Let us all beware, however, not to place new obstacles along that way. We must avoid developments in doctrine and in ecumenical relationships that would hinder our progress toward the unity we seek. At the same time, we have to be sure that our attitudes, our words, our devotions, and our understandings respect fully the truths we have set out so clearly in the *Joint Declaration*.

Third, we are reminded by the *Joint Declaration* of the new life that we have received, not through any merit of ours, but through the free gift of Jesus Christ. This is cause for constant thanksgiving and celebration—something that we can and should do together far more often than in the past. It is good to remember also that what we have achieved in the *Joint Declaration* is not primarily the result of the efforts of those involved, but of the grace that comes to us from the Holy Spirit. Prayer has played an important role and prayer for unity continues to be an essential part of our ongoing relations.

And then, fourth, we are also reminded of our responsibility to live fully the new life that has been so freely given to us. Catholics and Lutherans are called to give witness to their faith in Christ to the world of the coming third Christian Millennium. As the Reverend Herbert Anderson has reminded us: "[W]e live in a time in which the pervasiveness of selfishness and greed and scapegoating necessitates more taking responsibility for our actions."[4] Justification calls for transformed living.

Together we can now proclaim to the world the same Good News of justification by faith in Christ. As I stated in July of 1997 before the Ninth Assembly of the Lutheran World Federation in Hong Kong:

> To those citizens of today who are so often the victims of false and questionable values created by materialism and secularization, Lutherans and Catholics can now confess together, in the words of the *Joint Declaration*, "that all persons depend completely on the saving grace of God for their salvation" (*JD* 19). To those who are broken-hearted, or feel overwhelmed by the manifold threats to life and to well being we can now confess together "that the faithful can rely on the mercy and promises of God" (*JD* 34). To those who feel deeply the burden of guilt for sins committed in the past, or of a sinful life today, we can now "confess together that God forgives sin by grace and at the same time frees

human beings from sin's enslaving power and imparts the gift of new life in Christ" (*JD* 22). To those citizens today who, as in the time of St. Paul, are looking for the unknown God, we can now "confess together that in baptism the Holy Spirit unites one with Christ, justifies, and truly renews the person" (*JD* 28), and "that persons are justified by faith in the gospel 'apart from works prescribed by the law' (Rom 3:28)" (*JD* 31).

To do this more effectively we need also to grow together in Christ. The *Joint Declaration* must not remain a document somewhere over there in Geneva and Rome. What we have achieved must become part of the lives of our parishes and congregations, wherever they are. How this can best be done needs to be studied and carried out at the local level. One suggestion that I would make is that the Bible studies on justification that the Lutheran World Federation and the Pontifical Council for Promoting Christian Unity prepared together a couple of years ago be taken up and reflected on jointly by Lutheran and Catholic congregations.

VI. Conclusions

The *Joint Declaration on the Doctrine of Justification* can be seen as a further sign that, as the Second Vatican Council's Decree on Ecumenism stated: "The Lord of Ages . . . wisely and patiently follows out the plan of his grace on our behalf, sinners that we are. In recent times he has begun to bestow more generously upon divided Christians remorse over their divisions and longing for unity."[5] With the *Joint Declaration* Catholics and Lutherans have reached a consensus that has not been achieved in 450 years. This is surely reason enough to look to the future with hope. And to continue our dialogue with courage.

This agreement between Lutherans and Catholics has been fashioned by decades of theological dialogue, supported by prayer for unity, and is a tribute to the persistence of the Lutheran World Federation and the Catholic Church. Yet we would surely be remiss if we did not acknowledge our firm conviction that accompanying all this were impulses fostered by the grace of the Holy Spirit, who is the Spirit of unity and who assists us in responding to the prayer of Jesus for his followers "that they may all be one" (John 17:21).

For my part, I conclude with the following words from the *Joint Declaration*, which I have the privilege to endorse once again:

> We give thanks to the Lord for this decisive step forward on the way to overcoming the division of the church. We ask the Holy Spirit to lead us further toward that visible unity which is Christ's will (*JD* 44).

Notes

[1] Harding Meyer and Lukas Vischer, eds., *Growth in Agreement* (New York/Ramsey: Paulist Press and Geneva: World Council of Churches, 1984) 168–89, and *Church and Justification* (Geneva: Lutheran World Federation, 1994).

[2] H. George Anderson, T. Austin Murphy and Joseph A. Burgess, eds., *Justification by Faith: Lutherans and Catholics in Dialogue VII* (Minneapolis: Augsburg Publishing House, 1985), and Karl Lehmann and Wolfhart Pannenberg, eds., *The Condemnations of the Reformation Era: Do They Still Divide?* trans. Margaret Kohl (Minneapolis: Augsburg Fortress, 1990). See also Karl Lehmann, Michael Root, and William G. Rusch, eds., *Justification by Faith: Do the Sixteenth-Century Condemnations Still Apply?* trans. Michael Root and William G. Rusch with original essays by Michael Root and William G. Rusch and J. Francis Stafford (New York: Continuum, 1997).

[3] The Rev. Father Raniero Cantalaamessa, O.M. CAP. (Manuscript, December 1999).

[4] Herbert Anderson, *Ecumenical Trends* 28/5 (1999) 5/69.

[5] Austin P. Flannery, ed., *Documents of Vatican II* (Grand Rapids, Mich.: Wm. B. Eerdmans Publishing Co., 1975) 452.

Chapter 8

Beyond Justification:
An Orthodox Perspective

Valerie A. Karras

Introduction

A search on the ATLA Religion Index for articles on the *Joint Dec-laration on the Doctrine of Justification* from an Orthodox perspective comes up empty. This is not surprising, and it is not due primarily to the recent date of the declaration. You see, while of course everyone re-joices to see two Western Churches overcome the mutual condemna-tions of several centuries, Orthodox in general have never quite understood what all the fuss was about to begin with.

Orthodox religious formation is similar, strangely enough, to Pen-tecostalism in its experiential and synergistic approach to salvation—there isn't much talk about justification. Moreover, this isn't something new to Orthodoxy. Eastern Christianity from its origins shows a sin-gular lack of interest in discussing its soteriology in terms of justifica-tion. (I should note here that *ressourcement*—retrieving early theology and tradition—is a constitutive part of an Orthodox theologian's makeup.)

Robert Eno has pointed out that the second generation of Chris-tians, the Apostolic Fathers, "have been seen as presenting an almost total disappearance of the Pauline point of view."[1] A search of Greek patristic literature in *Thesaurus Linguae Graecae* shows that, over a pe-riod of a couple of centuries that includes the theologically rich fourth century, most Greek Fathers don't talk much about δικαιοσύνη ("justi-fication" or "righteousness") except when exegeting a passage using that term. The striking exception is Gregory of Nyssa, the late fourth-century bishop who was younger brother to Basil of Caesarea, but, interestingly, when Gregory uses the term, it is almost always in the context of the true, Christian way of life, in other words, works of righteousness; neither Nyssa nor any other Eastern Father ever writes in terms of what Lutheranism calls "forensic justification" (some would claim that the mid-fourth-century Alexandrian bishop Athanasius did, but we will return to this issue later).

The absence in Eastern Christianity of a soteriology in terms of forensic justification is serious because Orthodoxy believes not only in ecumenism across geographical space, but especially "ecumenism in time," i.e., the need to be consistent with the theological tradition of the Church from the earliest centuries.[2] Thus, the traditional Orthodox mind is immediately suspicious of biblical interpretations that have little or no root in the early life and theology of the Church; this is true in spades particularly of the forensic notion of justification, and of its consequent bifurcation of faith and works. *Sola scriptura* means little to the Orthodox, who as opposed to placing Scripture *over* the Church, have a full sense of Scripture's crucial but interrelated place *within* the Church's continuing life: the apostolic Church communities which produced many of the books of the New Testament, the communities of the Catholic Church which over a period of centuries determined which books circulating through various communities truly encapsulated the elements of the apostolic faith; the dogmas and Creed declared by the whole Church in response to the frequent controversies over the nature of the Trinity and of the *theanthropos* Jesus Christ, controversies which frequently arose precisely from dueling perspectives of which biblical texts were normative and of how those texts should be interpreted.

This of course does not mean that the Orthodox do not believe that each generation of Christians may receive new insights into Scripture, especially insights relevant in a given cultural context. However, it does mean that the new insights must remain consistent with earlier ones, and that one or two Pauline passages (and one specific interpretation of those passages) are not considered theologically normative—particularly as a foundation for a soteriological dogma—unless the early and continuing tradition of the Church show them consistently to have been viewed as such.[3]

History is important in a second way. Because of its less juridical exegesis of Pauline soteriological statements, Eastern Christianity has never had anything approaching the kind of faith v. works controversies that have enveloped and (for both good and ill) theologically shaped the Christian West, whether one considers the late fourth-/early fifth-century Pelagian controversy or the sixteenth-century Protestant Reformation begun by Martin Luther.[4] Rather, the East has maintained a somewhat distant and even puzzled attitude toward the theological polemics which have raged over justification in terms of faith or works.

For example, in Jerusalem around the year 415, neither Jerome nor a Spanish priest named Orosius was able to persuade the Holy City's bishop, John, and his synod to condemn Pelagius, who was also living in Jerusalem at the time.[5] John saw the controversy as a concern of the Latin Church solely and, quite frankly, appeared not to understand what the hullabaloo was all about. Equally revealing of the East's attitude toward the controversy is the fact that Caelestius, one of Pelagius' chief advocates (and perhaps more Pelagian than Pelagius himself), went to Ephesus to be ordained when his rejection of the doctrine of original guilt made his candidacy in Carthage unacceptable.

A millennium later, in the exchange of theological correspondence between Ecumenical Patriarch Jeremias II and the Lutheran theologians of the University of Tübingen in the 1570s,[6] Jeremias agreed with certain Lutheran theological views but disagreed on crucial issues concerning human free will and the place of works in justification, seemingly mystified by the disjuncture between faith and works expressed by the Augsburg Confession and the Reformers' letters. Modern bilateral dialogues between Orthodox and Lutheran churches have often focused on these same two issues.

To the Orthodox, the Western Church's convulsions over the nature of justification, and particularly the relationship between faith and works, are largely incomprehensible because the presuppositions underlying the debates are often alien to the Eastern Christian mind. The Christian East espouses a different theological anthropology from most of Western Christianity—both Catholic and Protestant—especially with respect to two elements of fallen human nature: original guilt and free will. The differences in these two anthropological concepts, in turn, contribute to differing soteriological understandings of, respectively, how Jesus Christ saves us (that is, what salvation means) and how we appropriate the salvation offered in Christ.

Therefore, we must examine these key concepts in Orthodox anthropology and soteriology, and their nexus in Christology, vis-à-vis their counterparts in traditional Western Christian theology. This will necessarily involve comparing different traditions' definitions and understandings of some key theological terms: sin, faith, salvation. Two contrasts recur: (1) the juridical approach of much of the West regarding sin and redemption, or restoration, versus the more existential and ontological approach of the East; and (2) the Western tendency to define, differentiate, and compartmentalize, as opposed to the Eastern tendency to theologize apophatically and, when cataphatically, primarily in a holistic and organic fashion. At the same time, some current trends are bringing the Catholic and especially the Lutheran communions closer to an Eastern Christian approach in these important areas.

Theological Anthropology: The Fall

1. Original Guilt

The Western Church tended to be more pessimistic about humankind's plight than was the Eastern Church; it taught a doctrine of original sin that included the conception of humankind's physical solidarity with Adam and its participation in Adam's sinful act. This was largely absent in Eastern thinking.[7]

> [A]ll men who are born according to the course of nature are conceived and born in sin. That is, all men are full of evil lust and inclinations from their mothers' wombs and are unable by nature to have true fear of God and true faith in God. Moreover, this inborn sickness and hereditary sin is truly sin.[8]

In order to discuss justification, one must first examine theological anthropology, specifically *postlapsarian*[9] theological anthropology; i.e., one cannot speak about how we are justified or saved in Christ without understanding what is wrong with us in our current state. The *Joint Declaration* does this as well, at the beginning of its explication of the common understanding (section 4). A comparison between the *Joint Declaration* and traditional Orthodox theology reveals immediate differences, in two distinct areas: (1) implicitly, the concept of inherited original guilt, and (2) explicitly, the understanding of free will, or human freedom.

All three traditions—Lutheran, Orthodox, and Roman Catholic—share a common general answer to the question of "What is wrong with humanity?"; all share an instinctive and biblical recognition that humanity lives outside of communion with God, that this lack of communion prevents us from being truly human, and that this state of separation from God is called, in shorthand, "sin." There are important differences, however, in the three traditions' understanding of how we have come to exist in this state, and how seriously it has affected our human nature; in other words, there are different theologies of "original sin."

Interestingly, the *Joint Declaration* sidesteps the question of original sin, perhaps because its meaning is hotly debated within confessions as well as between confessions. For instance, Lutheran theologian Carl Volz, while noting that "[s]ome Lutherans have leaned toward the traducianism of Tertullian,"[10] maintains that the Lutheran Confessions "do not develop a doctrine of the imputation of Adam's sin to his progeny. Rather, the fact of the universal relationship of all individuals in sin results in a community of sin."[11] Fellow Lutheran theologian Joseph Sittler has compared original sin to "a kind of pail which we've drained of the old literal statements and refilled with quite new interpretations. . . . [W]e no longer buy the old notion of biological transmission or try to have a system of inheritance."[12] Similarly reworked interpretations of original sin have been posited by Roman Catholic theologians as well.[13]

But Augustinian postlapsarian theological anthropology is built precisely on a notion of biological transmission, and many Western Christian confessions, while not articulating Augustine's anthropology to its logical extreme, nevertheless base their soteriology on its main outlines. Thus, "original sin" or, more precisely, "original guilt," is clearly a key element of theological anthropology and hence of soteriology. It is important therefore to note that Eastern Christianity distinguishes itself from Western Christianity, especially in its strictest Augustinian forms, in its rejection of any notion of inherited original guilt, that is, the idea that all humans share the guilt of Adam's sin.

This concept of original guilt, already visible in the theology of the third-century North African Latin Fathers Cyprian of Carthage and Tertullian, was developed in the early fifth century primarily by Augustine, who reacted to Pelagius' claim that infants need not be baptized since they have committed no personal sins. Augustine countered Pelagius by arguing from common Church practice and mixing it with traducianism via Romans 5:12: "sin came into the world through one man and death spread through sin, and so death spread to all men because [literally, 'in that' or 'in which'] all men sinned."[14] To briefly summarize Augustine's argument, which originated in

Cyprian: The Church universally baptized infants; therefore, since baptism confers remission of sins, and since infants have committed no personal sins, the Church baptizes infants obviously in order to remit the original sin which they inherit from Adam because all of humanity was seminally present in Adam.

While the Christian East consistently recognizes the effects of the "ancestral sin" in terms of human mortality, corruption (*phthora*), and a difficulty in maintaining an unwavering communion with God (the Eastern Fathers don't really speak in terms of "concupiscence"), it has never accepted Augustine's argument that all humanity inherits the guilt of Adam. Gregory of Nazianzus, fellow Cappadocian and best friend of Basil of Caesarea,[15] is one of the few Eastern Fathers to express any notion of inherited original sin. However, it would be difficult to ascribe to him a true theology of original sin since, as William Rusch remarks, Gregory "teaches in some passages in such a way as to rule out any doctrine of original sin and on other occasions he speaks of the involvement of all human beings in Adam's sin and fall (*Orations* 40,23; 33,9)."[16] John Chrysostom, archbishop of Constantinople and a contemporary of Augustine, in his *Homilies on Romans*, interprets Romans 5:12 simply to explain human mortality: "having once fallen, even they that had not eaten of the tree did from [Adam], all of them, become mortal."[17] In other words, the Greek Fathers saw the relationship between Adam and his descendants as organic and existential in nature with the notion of an inherited "guilt." We inherit the same mortal and corrupt nature which Adam possessed because of the Fall, but we do not inherit the guilt of that original sin which changed our human nature.[18]

Actually, the East finds slightly repugnant the notion that God would consider someone guilty of something which he or she did not do personally. Yet the Eastern Church, like the Western Church, baptizes infants. The East's insistence on infant baptism and simultaneous denial of original guilt is possible because Orthodoxy rejects Augustine's leap of logic regarding the purpose of infant baptism—the remission of sins. The Eastern Church of course recognizes the importance of baptism in washing away one's personal sins. However, that is not the only effect of baptism. As Carl Volz has noted for the Lutheran practice of infant baptism,[19] it grafts the baptized person, including infants, onto the Body of Christ and confers the gift of the Holy Spirit. This existential, ecclesiological understanding of baptism is clear in Chrysostom's *Third Baptismal Instruction*, where he states:

Although many men think that the only gift [baptism] confers is the re-mission of sins, we have counted its honors to the number of ten. It is on this account that we baptize even infants, although they are sinless, that they may be given the further gifts of sanctification, justice, filial adoption, and inheritance, that they may be brothers and members of Christ, and become dwelling places of the Spirit.[20]

This is borne out in the differing sacramental practices of the Western and Eastern Churches. The West, both Catholic and Lutheran, traditionally has withheld chrismation (or confirmation) and Holy Communion for some years after baptism, and frequently separates confirmation and communion from each other by several years as well. This sacramental practice is consistent with a soteriology which distinguishes between *justification* (baptism) and *sanctification* (chrismation or confirmation).[21] However, the Eastern Church has continued the early Church's practice of regarding baptism and chrismation as one rite of initiation—remission of sins and concurrently the beginning of sanctification, i.e., incorporation into both the Body of Christ and the life of the Holy Spirit. Moreover, as Patriarch Jeremias noted,[22] the Orthodox Church acts sacramentally in a manner consistent with this theology: the baptized person, even if an infant, is incorporated into the *full* sacramental and spiritual life of the Church, i.e., the Orthodox Church communes baptized infants as full members of the Church.

This existential understanding of the purpose of baptism as the beginning of one's life in Christ *through the seal of the gift of the Holy Spirit* differs substantially from the juridically rooted emphasis on sin characteristic of the West. It is true that Pelagius spoke of infant baptism in terms of entrance into the kingdom of heaven, yet apparently he did not see its primary importance. As for Augustine, the contrast with Chrysostom is sharp: they are writing only a few years apart, and yet their understandings of the purpose of infant baptism are light-years apart. This is why, from the Orthodox point of view, Augustine's and Pelagius' arguments are simply flip sides of the same coin. Both operate under the assumption that the primary purpose of baptism — in fact, virtually the sole purpose as far as their debate is concerned—is the remission of sins. The Orthodox approach sees the death of the old man (the work of the Cross) only through the lens of the rebirth of the new man (the life of the Resurrection), an organic view which shall be seen again later.

2. Free Will and the Imago Dei

The question of original sin, or what humanity lost in the Fall, is related to the question of what God gave humanity in the act of creation and what humanity retains even in its fallen state. For the Greek Fathers, this spiritual capacity of human nature is encapsulated in the language of Genesis 1:26-7: God created humanity according to God's own "image." Furthermore, both the Eastern Church and the medieval Latin Church distinguished between the "image of God" (Latin *imago Dei*) and the "likeness" or similitude of God, based on the differences between Genesis 1:26 and 1:27. The image designated the potential or capabilities inherent in all human beings, i.e., qualities such as reason; the likeness meant true likeness (at the level of human existence, of course) to God, the realization of human potential as the perpetual fulfillment of a dynamic process between the human person and God. The Greek Fathers in particular developed a generous anthropology around the concept of the *imago Dei*, even for postlapsarian human nature; as Gregory of Nyssa states in his *Sixth Homily on the Beatitudes*, the divine imprint may be obscured but it is still intact.[23] The anthropology of the Roman Church, influenced by Augustine, was less generous than that of the East, but still accented human capacity.

By contrast, classical Lutheran thought presented a sharp break with the general tenor of biblical interpretation of Genesis 1:26-7 in both the Eastern and Western forms of early and medieval Christianity. As Robert Wilken has shown,[24] Luther, Melanchthon, and others rejected the distinction drawn by most early and medieval theologians, Latin and Greek alike, between image and likeness.[25] As we shall see later, this rejection has consequences for (or, perhaps is itself a consequence of) the Reformers' soteriology. Moreover, Lutherans from Martin Luther himself to later writers such as the eighteenth-century theologian John Gerhard have interpreted the *imago Dei* largely in a negative sense: it encapsulates what humanity lost in the Fall.[26] Wilken argues that Luther "did not . . . abandon the image entirely and was willing to say that it remained after the fall,"[27] and that "the Lutheran tradition stands within the broad stream of patristic and medieval tradition that saw freedom of the will, reason, human responsibility . . . as marks of the divine image. This image was not lost, but only tarnished in the fall."[28] Nevertheless, he admits that Luther describes the "marks of the image" (memory, will, and mind) as "most depraved and most seriously weakened, yes, to put it more clearly, they are utterly leprous and unclean,"[29] and quotes Gerhard as asserting that "to deny that the image of God has been lost is to deny original sin itself."[30]

The question of the *imago Dei* is significant because it is here that East and West disagree on a second important element of theological anthropology: free will. While Orthodoxy maintains that free will is a constitutive element of the *imago Dei*, both Roman Catholicism and Lutheranism—sharing an Augustinian heritage—assert that one of the aspects of original sin is the loss of free will with respect to humanity's orientation toward God. Human freedom was one of the issues at the heart of the fifth-century Western Christian debate over faith and works, i.e., over the relative divine and human contributions to salvation. The Western Christian historical context has caused many theologians, particularly evangelical Protestant theologians, to experience great difficulty thinking "outside the box" of the Western either/or approach to this topic. For instance, at a 1999 conference sponsored by the Society for the Study of Evangelicalism and Eastern Orthodoxy, J. I. Packer distributed a copy of some course materials. I noted that under the topic of faith and works he listed the Orthodox as "semi-Pelagian." He was "semi-right." As Bishop Kallistos (Ware) of Diokleia proclaimed at the beginning of his 1998 Bellarmine Lecture at Saint Louis University, "I suppose I should tell you straightaway that I am an Arminian." Ware's comment was amusing but also truthful because, in Eastern Christian soteriology, human freedom plays an important role, but not as Pelagian foil to Augustinian determinism.

At the heart of the Orthodox understanding of what constitutes the *imago Dei* in the human person, even after the Fall, lies the concept of free will. This is perhaps best seen in the theology of Gregory of Nyssa. In his seminal work *On the Making of the Human Person*, Nyssa lists a variety of traits which characterize the divine image in humanity, but asserts that

> pre-eminent among all is the fact that we are free from necessity, and not in bondage to any natural power, but have decision in our own power as we please; for virtue is a voluntary thing, subject to no dominion: that which is the result of compulsion and force cannot be virtue.[31]

Over a thousand years later, Jeremias II, patriarch of Constantinople, would take up this refrain in his response to the Lutheran theologians of Tübingen regarding the Augsburg Confession. First, Jeremias quotes at length from Chrysostom's *Twelfth Homily on the Epistle to the Hebrews*, where the Antiochene Father asserts that "All indeed depends on God, but not so that our free-will is hindered. . . . For we must first choose the good; and then He leads us to His own. He does not anticipate our choice, lest our free-will should be outraged. But when we have chosen, then great is the assistance he brings to us."[32] Linking the concepts of sin and virtue to free will in a manner similar to Nyssa, Jeremias sets the stage for his discussion of faith and works by averring:

> I declare that everyone is capable of virtue. For whatever a person is not able to do, he is not able to do even if forced. But if a person is able when forced to do what he is not doing, then it is by his own choice that he is not doing it.[33]

Certainly, Eastern Christianity recognizes that humanity has lost an element of its freedom in its subjection to the "passions" (understood as spiritual as well as physical needs and desires). This is particularly emphasized in ascetic writings. However, despite recognition of the difficulty in consistently exercising one's freedom properly, Eastern Christian thought is virtually unanimous from the earliest centuries in affirming humanity's fundamental freedom to do good or ill, to turn toward God or away from him. By contrast, the Christian West, both Roman Catholic and Protestant, has been strongly influenced by Augustine's peculiarly negative concept of free will. Luther is a prime example: "After the fall of Adam, free-will is a mere expression; whenever it acts in character, it commits mortal sin."[34] The classical Western view is summed up in the very title of section 4.1 of the *Joint Declaration*—"Human Powerlessness and Sin in Relation to Justification." According to Lutheran teaching, "human beings are incapable of cooperating in their salvation, because *as sinners they actively oppose God* and his saving action [emphasis added]."[35] In the previous paragraph of the *Joint Declaration*, the Roman Catholic position presents a more positive assessment of the human response to God, yet it too undercuts the human will by interpreting this human response as essentially divine, not human: "When Catholics say that persons 'cooperate' in preparing for and accepting justification by consenting to God's justifying action, they see such personal consent as itself an effect of grace, *not as an action arising from innate human abilities* [emphasis added]."[36] Catholics and Lutherans together assert in the *Joint Declaration* that humans "are incapable of turning by themselves to God to seek deliverance."[37] So, although certain bilateral dialogues with the Orthodox have tried to present a stronger sense of free human responsiveness, both positive and negative,[38] the understanding of faith for Lutherans especially is not based on human freedom:

[F]aith is the awareness worked by the Spirit that salvation is not from us, but for us. Faith is not the response of a person's free will to choose the grace of God. The [Lutheran] confessions slam the door on free will to keep out every possible synergistic intrusion. They reject the statement used by some of the ancient Fathers that God draws, but draws the person who is willing. Instead, God makes unwilling persons willing to do the will of Christ.[39]

Thus, neither the Lutheran nor the Roman Catholic understanding of justification includes a truly human component. The negative anthropology of both negates human freedom because it excludes an inherent desire for and ability to turn toward God in humanity's fallen condition. Consequently, the Christian West, following Augustine, developed the idea of prevenient grace: a human being can only turn toward God after God has first imparted to him or her a special grace which allows the person to recognize and respond to God.[40] If one also hypothesizes that God may not choose to bestow this prevenient grace on all human beings, then one comes naturally to the theory of election or predestination present in Augustine's later anti-Pelagian works and resurrected full force in the Reformed Protestantism of Calvin as well as in such branches of Lutheranism as the Missouri Synod.[41] Happily, the *Joint Declaration* affirms that "[a]ll people are called by God to salvation in Christ."[42]

Eastern Christianity counters this negative view of postlapsarian human nature with the positive theological anthropology enshrined in the Christology of the Sixth Ecumenical Council, held in Constantinople in 680–81. The council was convoked to deal with an attempt to underscore the unity of the person of Jesus Christ by declaring that he had only one will, his divine will, hence, the heresy was named *Monotheletism*. In rejecting Monotheletism, the council articulated a Christology based on the theological anthropology of the brilliant seventh-century Greek theologian Maximos the Confessor. Maximos distinguished between (1) the "natural" human will, which is a characteristic of human nature; it is oriented toward God and *continues to exist and operate even after the Fall*, and (2) the "gnomic" will, a personal property, or personal mode of expressing the natural will which is peculiar to fallen human beings and is characterized by opinion and deliberation because the fallen human person lacks true knowledge of where the Good lies.[43]

Maximos asserted that self-determination (literally, *self-determined movement*) is a constitutive element of human nature, but is not aimless;

our natural free will is oriented toward God precisely because humanity is created *by* God, in *his* image. A special act of God's grace (i.e., prevenient grace) is not required for us to orient ourselves toward him; orientation toward God is at the heart of our human nature. Thus, Maximos' theological anthropology, based on the conviction that the *imago Dei* is retained in postlapsarian human nature, assumes that human beings retain a natural orientation toward God.[44] In part, this is why human freedom plays such a central role in Eastern Christian theology "without the problematic character that it ha[s] in Western writers."[45] Interestingly, Western Christianity claims to affirm the Christology of the Sixth Ecumenical Council. However, it is impossible to accept Maximos' Christology without accepting equally the anthropology on which it is based, namely his concept of the natural human will which Christ assumes as part of his fallen human nature.

With respect, then, to the soteriological question of "What is wrong with humanity in its fallen state?" the problem of the human condition is not, as it is conceived in Western Christianity, that human beings have no natural orientation toward God. The problem of our fallen condition is that, because we have broken communion with God, our spiritual vision has become "clouded" so that we fail to recognize clearly in what direction our natural orientation lies and therefore fail to move consistently in that direction, i.e., to restore communion with God.

Thus, Orthodoxy understands human sin primarily not as deliberate and willful opposition to God, but rather as an inability to know ourselves and God clearly. It is as though God were calling out to us and coming after us in a storm, but we thought we heard his voice in another direction and kept moving away from him, either directly or obliquely. It is illuminating that the Greek word for sin, *hamartia*, means "to miss the mark." Despite our orientation toward God, we "miss the mark" because, not only does the clouded spiritual vision of our fallen condition make it difficult for us to see God clearly, but we fail to understand even ourselves truly; thus, we constantly do things which make us feel only incompletely and unsatisfactorily good or happy because we don't recognize that God is himself the fulfillment of our innate desire and natural movement. Explaining Maximos' theology, Andrew Louth offers, "with fallen creatures, their own nature has become opaque to them, they no longer know what they want, and experience coercion in trying to love what cannot give fulfilment."[46] Ultimately, it is not our natural human will that is deficient, but rather how we perceive it and the way, or mode, by which we express it; as Louth sourly opines, "it is a frustrating and confusing business."[47]

Soteriology—Justification and Sanctification, or Sharing and Deification

1. Restoration of Fallen Humanity—Justification As "Sharing"

Having examined the problem of "What's wrong with humanity?" it is appropriate now to consider the soteriological solution which dominates the *Joint Declaration*, i.e., "What will make humanity right?," or, more specifically, "How does Jesus Christ make humanity right?" The first thing to note is that the ecumenical councils made no dogmatic definitions explicitly on soteriology alone. However, in the medieval Latin Church, the satisfaction theory of atonement gained currency, and the penitential system (temporal punishment is still required of human beings even for forgiven sins) arising from it, which is still part of the theology and practice of the Roman Church, led to an "opposite reaction" in the justification soteriology of Martin Luther. And, by insisting on "justification by grace alone, received through faith alone," by enshrining it in such creeds as the Augsburg Confession, and by "'proclaim[ing] this as the doctrine by which the Church "stands or falls"' (*articulis stantis et cadentis ecclesiae*),"[48] the partisans of the Reformation, as thoroughly as the medieval Latin theologians, dogmatized a particular soteriology.

Meanwhile, as noted in the introduction, Eastern Christianity never developed either a doctrine of forensic justification or a real atonement soteriology (and certainly nothing akin to the theory of "satisfaction" proposed by Anselm in the twelfth century). In other words, Orthodox soteriology stands outside the juridical approach of Western Christianity, both Roman Catholic and Protestant.[49] Rather, it is based deeply and consistently on the theology of the ecumenical councils; in particular, on the Christology articulated in the ecumenical councils. For, while no doctrinal statements of what effects (or causes) salvation are articulated in the ecumenical councils, one cannot truly grasp the logic and significance of the christological definitions except insofar as one understands the soteriological issues (and, hence anthropological issues) which lie behind them.[50]

Thus, Eastern Christian soteriology constitutes a challenge to Bernhard Lohse's claim that Luther's doctrine of justification expresses "the Christology of the ancient church":

> In Luther, Christology and soteriology are intimately connected with each other, as they are in Athanasius, or Cyril of Alexandria, except that Luther makes the connection much more explicit. Christology is realized in the doctrine of justification, and the doctrine of justification is nothing else but a summary of Christology in soteriological perspective.[51]

The insight that Christology and soteriology are integrally linked is important. After all, the ecumenical councils were not interested in producing esoteric christological texts for speculative theologians with an arcane interest in the nature of Jesus Christ. The bishops of these councils recognized the soteriological significance of the christological issues raised in the fourth through ninth centuries. And, there is no doubt that Christology is integrally linked to Luther's soteriology.

The question is whether Luther's soteriology—and, for that matter, other forms of Western atonement soteriology—are truly based on the Christology of the early Fathers, especially those behind the dogmatic formulations of the ecumenical councils. Both the dogmatic definitions and the supplementary patristic writings surrounding the christological controversies seem to indicate a negative answer to the question. Far from emphasizing atonement as satisfaction or a forensic notion of justification, these writings express an understanding of human salvation rooted not simply in a particular activity of Jesus Christ,[52] but in the very *person* of Jesus Christ. Gregory of Nyssa, writing more than a millennium before the development of the Lutheran doctrine of "imputed righteousness," in the context of the controversy over the extreme form of Arianism known as Eunomianism, rejects the notion that one could be "totally righteous" in a legal but not existential sense. Human beings are not restored to communion with God through an act of spiritual prestidigitation where God looks and thinks he sees humanity, but in fact is really seeing his Son.[53] Justification must be as organic and existential as sin is:

> Humanity's justification through forgiveness of sins is not a mere covering over man's sins, but a real destruction of them. It is not a mere external decision but a reality. Sins are forgiven truly and really. God does not declare someone to be justified if he [or she] is not really free. We understand this teaching better if we remember the relation between Adam and Christ. As we became not only apparently but really sinful because of Adam, so through Christ the Second Adam we become really justified.[54]

This emphasis on the *personal* christological nature of soteriology is particularly evident in the Second, Fourth, Sixth, and Seventh Ecumenical Councils.[55] These four councils insisted on the full humanity of Christ not because it was simply "fitting" for God to become fully human in order to "pay the price" for other humans, but because it was ontologically *necessary* for God to become human. Thus, Gregory of Nazianzus, the presider and theological leader of the Second Ecumenical Council, described what the *Joint Declaration* calls "justification" in terms of the healing of our fallen human nature through Christ's sharing of that same fallen human nature: "For that which He has not assumed He has not healed; but that which is united to His Godhead is also saved."[56] It is this same soteriological consideration which informs both the anthropology and the Christology of Maximos the Confessor three hundred years later, and which causes iconophile authors such as John of Damascus and Theodore of Studios in the eighth and ninth century, respectively, to recognize that an unwillingness to depict Jesus Christ in the flesh amounted to a denial of the reality of the Incarnation and hence threatened the entire framework of salvation.

In other words, the christological definitions of the ecumenical councils are grounded in a relational-ontological soteriology based on humanity's being *homoousios* (one in essence, substance, or nature) in our humanity with Jesus Christ, who is in turn *homoousios* with God the Father. Thus, the soteriology of the ecumenical councils (and hence of Eastern Christianity) is based not on putting us juridically "right" with God, but on the existential healing of human nature through the person of Jesus Christ. As Bishop Kallistos Ware notes in his introduction to Orthodox theology and spirituality, *The Orthodox Way*, Orthodox soteriology is inescapably linked to Christology and may be described "salvation as sharing."[57]

Lucian Turcescu[58] has rightly criticized Orthodoxy for focusing so strongly on *theosis* that it has tended to ignore the "justification" side of the coin. However, I disagree with him that, simply because Jewish notions of justification had forensic significance, therefore Paul, or the early Church, understood the term in the same legalistic way (in fact, Paul's point in Romans is precisely to rid Jewish Christians of their forensic understanding of justification rooted in the Levitical law). Orthodoxy may emphasize *theosis* (correlated to "sanctification" in the Lutheran model) and see one continuous relational process between the human person and God,[59] but it does not ignore the distinction between justification and sanctification. Rather, the Eastern Church recognizes *two* purposes to the Incarnation, which may be identified with justification and sanctification: restoring human nature to its prelapsarian state or "justification" and providing the possibility for true union with God through participation, respectively. The former purpose was necessitated by the Fall and has been the focus of Western soteriology. For the East the restoration of human nature to its prelapsarian potential (justification) explains why the Son of God took on humanity's *fallen* human nature, i.e., why it was necessary for Christ to die and be resurrected. Hence, Orthodoxy agrees in affirming the free nature of that restoration through grace (in fact, Orthodoxy proclaims the gratuitous nature of our justification even more strongly than most of Western Christianity since it is given to *all* humanity, not just the "elect" or those receiving prevenient grace).[60] However, the Fall is not the primary reason for the Incarnation itself since, as Maximos and others point out, the Incarnation was always part of God's plan since it was the means by which humanity could truly achieve salvation, understood as *theosis* or union with God, an approach which will be discussed in more detail in the following section.

The Cross thus acquires ontological rather than forensic significance.[61] This is why juridical notions of atonement and justification cannot truly be reconciled with the soteriology underlying the Christology of the ecumenical councils. John Breck identified this as the primary reason why Eastern soteriology never developed along Western lines: "none of the traditional Western theories of justification, atonement, etc., really necessitates personal divine involvement in the death that accomplishes our redemption."[62] In other words, the soteriology implicit in the christological definitions of the ecumenical councils is based on the assumption that Christ saves us primarily by *who* he is as opposed to *what* he does, although the importance of the latter is affirmed as well, e.g., in the Nicene Creed, without however defining the exact manner in which his actions were salvific.

Thus, as many theologians have noted, the Orthodox understanding of Christ's crucifixion, derived from soteriological Christology, is diametrically opposed to the Anselmian theory of satisfaction which underpins both Catholic and Lutheran notions of justification. God is not a judge in a courtroom, and Christ did not pay the legal penalty or "fine" for our sins. His redemptive work was not completed on the cross, with the Resurrection as a nice afterword. The eternal Son of God took on our fallen human nature, including our mortality, in order to restore it to the possibility of immortality. Jesus Christ died *so that* he might be resurrected. Just as Christ is *homoousios* with the Father in his divinity, we are *homoousios* with him in his humanity; it is through our sharing of his crucified *and* resurrected human nature that our own human nature is transformed from mortality to immortality. John Meyendorff summarizes the significance of the Cross for the Christian East as follows:

> In the East, the Cross is envisaged not so much as the punishment of the just one, which "satisfies" a transcendent Justice requiring a retribution for [one's] sins. As George Florovsky rightly puts it: "the death on the Cross was effective, not as a death of an Innocent One, but as the death of the Incarnate Lord." The point was not to satisfy a legal requirement, but to vanquish the frightful cosmic reality of death, which held humanity under its usurped control and pushed it into the vicious circle of sin and corruption.[63]

The limited atonement, satisfaction, or justification language in certain Greek Fathers, such as Athanasius,[64] read within these Fathers' broader theological framework, are thus recognized not as reified doctrinal statements supporting Western atonement soteriologies that would not fully develop for close to or even more than a millennium yet, but as metaphors for an existentialist soteriology of sharing. The dramatically different nature of this ontological soteriology, grounded in the Christology of the ecumenical councils, explains why, as the "Common Statement" from the American Lutheran-Orthodox dialogues notes, "the Orthodox have been uneasy with medieval Western formulations that conceive of Christ's atonement as a 'satisfaction' for sins."[65]

2. Beyond Justification—Salvation As Deification

This ontological approach to our redemption in Christ has at least two important implications with respect to the *Joint Declaration*. First, justification, as has been seen, is understood not in a juridical sense but in an existential sense; hence, as mentioned above, God's initiative and action in the creation of humanity according to his image, and in the Incarnation, Cross, and Resurrection are of *universal* significance to humanity and *cosmic* significance to creation as a whole.[66] Orthodoxy understands justification in Christ as restoring to *all* humanity the potential for immortality and communion with God lost in the Fall. This is because all human beings share the human nature of Jesus Christ, which was restored in the resurrection. Christ's incarnation, passion, and resurrection thus serve as a restoration of the potential of prelapsarian human nature.

However, whether or not human beings avail themselves of the redemption and restoration offered in Christ is dependent on how they exercise their human freedom by responding positively to union with Christ. As Maximos the Confessor demonstrated and the Fathers of the Sixth Ecumenical Council implicitly affirmed, orientation toward God and the freedom to act on it are inherent in human nature. John Breck observes that, while God is the one who initiates, "the objects of that initiative—humanity and the cosmos—are neither passive nor static. By virtue of created nature, humanity possesses an inner, dynamic capacity for response, one that engages the entire cosmos of which humanity is the microcosm."[67]

But, secondly, Eastern Christianity's "sharing" soteriology, because of its relational nature, does not equate salvation with justification alone, particularly justification conceived in a juridical fashion ("imputed righteousness"). The first section of the *Joint Declaration* acknowledges the numerous biblical facets of the term justification or righteousness, including its spiritual, ethical, and sacramental significance but does not integrate this broad spectrum fully into the third and fourth sections ("The Common Understanding of Justification" and "Explicating the Common Understanding of Justification," respectively).

Orthodoxy conceives of justification broadly, and of salvation more broadly still—as a relationship and an organic process, not as an event or static state of being. This is, in part, because "it was clear that the Eastern Fathers regarded salvation as more than simply a restoration of what had been lost in the first Adam. For whatever the final consummation brought, it had to incorporate what had been won in the second Adam."[68] In other words, salvation in Christ means more than a return to the prelapsarian human existence of Paradise. From the perspective of Irenaeus of Lyons, for example, Adam and Eve were spiritual infants. Salvation must encompass not only healing but also spiritual development and maturity.

To approach this idea from another angle, Genesis 1:26-27, because it forms the basis for Eastern Christian anthropology, consequently is normative for its soteriology as well. Summarizing an earlier section, humanity, according to Genesis 1:27, is created *in the image* of God but, based on Genesis 1:26, it is created to *become* the image *and likeness* of God. The likeness of God, however, is not understood in an ethical sense, i.e., as simply acquiring "virtues." Eastern

Christianity is not Pelagian in the sense it is typically understood in the West; that is, human beings cannot acquire the divine likeness through human-initiated and -dominated activity. Rather, growing into the divine likeness—living an ever more authentic human existence—means *communion* and *union* with God. As Meyendorff observes, "'natural' human life presupposes communion with God."[69] Again, Irenaeus of Lyons, a disciple once removed from John the Evangelist, is instructive. Meyendorff explains the double significance of the Incarnation for Irenaeus, viewed through his dynamic anthropology of spiritual maturation and his soteriology of recapitulation in Christ, in the following way:

> This approach implies that in Christ there was a restoration of the true human nature, not an external addition of "grace" to an otherwise autonomous human existence. Salvation does not consist in an extrinsic "justification"—although this "legal" dimension is fully legitimate whenever one approaches salvation within the Old Testament category of the fulfillment of the law (as Paul does in Romans and Galatians)—but in a renewed communion with God, making human life fully human again.[70]

This Eastern Christian understanding of communion or union with God connotes a true union which, like the appearance of Christ on Mt. Tabor, transfigures and *deifies* our human nature. In one of the most succinct and explicit articulations of this doctrine, known as *theosis* (deification),[71] Athanasius declared, "He [the Logos] became man that we might be deified."[72] Similarly, in his *Defense of the Nicene Definition*, the Alexandrian bishop asserted:

> . . . the Word was made flesh in order to offer up this body for all, and that we[,] partaking of His Spirit, might be deified[,] a gift which we could not otherwise have gained than by His clothing Himself in our created body, for hence we derive our name of "[people] of God" and "[people] in Christ."[73]

As William Rusch has demonstrated,[74] this concept of salvation as *theosis* is consistently evident in the early writings of the Christian East: implicitly in the letters of Ignatius of Antioch, and explicitly in the writings of second- and early third-century theologians such as Irenaeus of Lyons,[75] Clement of Alexandria,[76] and Origen,[77] as well as later in the fourth-century Athanasius and the Cappadocians, and later still in Pseudo-Dionysius and Maximos the Confessor.

The doctrine of deification is a direct consequence of an incarnational, hence ontological, soteriology. *Theosis* is not just the "goal" of salvation; it *is* salvation in its essence and fulfillment. Orthodox theologian John Breck argues:

> If the *telos* of human existence were less than a total sharing in triune life—if people were called, for example, to mere "fellowship" with God through justification or even to eternal enjoyment of the "beatific vision"—then it would have been theoretically possible for God to work out salvation without resorting to a true incarnation that required the eternal divine Logos to accept death in his assumed humanity. Full ontological participation of God in our human life is necessary if we are to know the same quality and degree of participation in his divine life.[78]

So, if understanding the soteriological significance of the incarnation as "justification" classically refers to the restoration of fallen human nature through Christ's death and resurrection, then the flip side of the Incarnation is the fulfillment of humanity's authentic existence in communion with God. Hence, Rusch identifies in Irenaeus' theology two images of the soteriological effect of Christ's incarnation: "one of salvation by sharing in Christ's human conquest of sin, the other salvation by participation in the nature of the divine Logos."[79]

Because the incarnation has a double significance—restoring humanity's prelapsarian human nature *and* making possible a deified human existence—it is not dependent on humanity's Fall. This is why Orthodoxy eschews the notion of *felix culpa*, the "happy fault" of Adam. Maximos the Confessor, for instance, articulates the concept of humanity as mediator or priest to all creation because its unique microcosmic makeup allows it to overcome and unite the various divisions existing in creation (e.g., between physical and spiritual). However, Maximos insists, only God himself is able to overcome the ultimate division—that between the Uncreated and the created, and he can do so only in his own Person.

> God becomes a human being, in order to save lost humanity. Through himself he has, in accordance with nature, united the fragments of the universal nature of the all . . . by which the union of the divided naturally comes about, and thus he fulfils the great purpose of God the Father, *to recapitulate everything both in heaven and earth in himself* (Eph. 1:10), *in whom everything has been created* (Col. 1:16).[80]

3. *Grace, Faith,* Theosis, *and the Finns*

To sum up the previous sections: Orthodoxy sees human nature as fallen and mortal, but as retaining its fundamental orientation toward God and not as inheriting some type of juridical guilt; we are redeemed from this fallen human nature by the incarnation of the Son of God, who assumes and shares this fallen, mortal nature in every aspect except sin, even unto death, restoring it to its former potentiality (i.e., "justifying" us) through his resurrection, in which we share. But restoration to the potentiality of Adam and Eve is just a starting point in Orthodox theology; we are called to communion with God, to grow and mature into the likeness of God, to become "deified" by participation in God's own life through the Holy Spirit.

Communion with God is of course a vital part of the spirituality of Western Christianity. Its soteriological significance, however, has been weaker in the West than in the East. Roman Catholic theology historically has been much closer than Lutheran theology to Orthodoxy in this regard with its doctrine of the "beatific vision." Its spirituality has been closer yet. That is, while much medieval Western spirituality is articulated in terms of true union with God,[81] medieval scholastic theology describes communion with God in terms that create a barrier between the human and the divine. Thomas Aquinas, for instance, develops through his epistemology a theology of participation in God which might be related to *theosis*.[82] However, as William Cavanaugh explains Aquinas's understanding of "participation," it excludes true union because Aquinas defines divine grace as created: "the participation of the Holy Spirit in us is 'created' charity."[83] Not surprisingly, it is the return to the Fathers at the heart of much of Catholicism's *nouvelle théologie* which helped to produce in the modern era theologians such as Henri de Lubac and Hans Urs von Balthasar, who provide an integralism between God and humanity found, in a slightly different way, in Karl Rahner as well.[84]

By contrast, the East never experienced Scholasticism. The continuous witness of the Eastern Church Fathers, from Origen and the Cappadocians to the fourteenth-century Byzantine monk and archbishop Gregory[85] is that grace is not "created" by God. It is God's own Being: not the divine essence, which remains utterly unknowable, but the divine *energies*, which are God's own self as immanent in creation. Palamas observes that there are three unions with or within the Divine: (1) essential union or union of essence, i.e., the Trinity; (2) personal union, i.e., the hypostatic union of the *theanthropos* Jesus Christ; and (3) participatory union, or union by participation, i.e., with God's energies. It is this third union which makes possible *theosis*—the deification of the human person. Thus, while the union between human and divine in Christ is qualitatively different (hypostatic as opposed to participatory) from that possible to us, Christ's transfigured human nature, revealed to the disciples on Mt. Tabor, serves as the model for realizing our full potential as human beings created for communion with God and who, while remaining always creatures, may be transformed into "divine creatures"[86] through grace, that is, through union with God's own energies.

If Roman Catholic theology differs markedly from Orthodoxy in respect to the created versus uncreated nature of grace and hence participation as presence versus participation as union, traditionally Lutheranism's doctrine of justification "by grace alone, through faith alone" has seemed even more removed from the Orthodox doctrine of salvation as deification. However, the work of several Finnish Lutheran scholars over the past two decades is doing much to revise that assessment.[87] Under the informal leadership of Tuomo Mannermaa, these theologians have reexamined the meaning of the word "faith" in the writings of Martin Luther, particularly in his earlier works. What they have uncovered has sparked controversy and shaken the foundations of Luther scholarship and of Lutheran thought. Faith, for Luther, is not primarily intellectual or emotional, nor is it something which God simply gives to us. Mannermaa and his disciples have latched onto the significance of Luther's expression, *"in ipsa fide Christus adest"* ("in faith itself Christ is present"). Faith, these Finnish scholars say, is for Luther nothing less than union with Christ. Mannermaa argues that Luther teaches justification or righteousness as inseparable from communion with God, *theosis*, in his *Lectures on Galatians*:

> "Christ who is grasped by faith and who lives in the heart is the Christian righteousness, on account of which God counts us righteous and gives us eternal life as gift.". . . At least on the level of terminology, the distinction, drawn in later Lutheranism, between justification as forgiveness and sanctification as divine indwelling, is alien to the Reformer. Forgiveness and indwelling of God are inseparable in the person of Christ . . .

In that sense, in Luther's theology, justification and *theosis* as participation in God are also inseparable.[88]

Moreover, fellow Finn Simo Peura notes that Luther abandoned the concept of created grace because the scholastic notion of habitual grace as an accident "did not go far enough to stress the ontological points that Luther wished to maintain."[89] Furthermore, Mannermaa discerns in the Formula of Concord (FC) divine indwelling—*inhabitatio Dei*—not simply as gift, but as reality.[90] Nevertheless, the FC distinguishes divine indwelling from justification and places it subsequent to it. In addition, Peura contends that the FC "excludes from gift everything else that according to Luther is included in it,"[91] and argues that the Formula of Concord falsely—and contrary to Luther's theology—divorces forensic justification (God's favor) from effective justification or sanctification (God's gift).[92]

Conclusion

Unfortunately, while the stimulating research by Mannermaa and company has found its way into the *Common Statement* of the American Lutheran-Orthodox dialogue, it is marginalized in the *Joint Declaration*.[93] It is true that the *Joint Declaration* was intended to treat the historical misconceptions of battling confessions regarding the understanding of justification and to underscore the inefficacy of human works to achieve salvation. Perhaps, then, the Finnish research on Luther as well as the hopeful recent discussion in the American Lutheran-Orthodox dialogue can help point the way to the next stage of bilateral and multilateral theological dialogue, that some of the differences in soteriological approach may be as seen more as the result of differing foci (particularly Luther's concern with humans before the judgment seat of Christ) than truly different understandings at the most fundamental level. From an Orthodox perspective, one of the most valuable contributions of the Finns is that, by spotlighting the nonexistential and nonrelational view of faith in forensic justification and by rediscovering within their own tradition an *ontological* relationship between soteriology and Christology through broadening justification to include *theosis*, they have moved Western Christian theology outside the differentiating, delineating, defining, compartmentalizing "box."[94] From an Orthodox perspective, continued movement *away from* a compartmentalized methodology and a juridical and passive anthropology and soteriology and *toward* a holistic methodology explicating a more generous anthropology and an existential, relational, synergistic soteriology would be welcome. Most of the pieces are there, but soteriology needs to be integrated not only more ontologically with Christology, but also with spirituality and sacramental theology. It is not coincidental that Eastern Christian theology is not articulated in philosophical syllogisms or biblical proof-texting; nor does it rely primarily on one or two figures (e.g., Augustine, Aquinas, Luther, Calvin). Orthodox theology, equally based with Catholicism and Lutheranism in Scripture and the ecumenical councils, is articulated through the personal and communal spiritual experiences of a number of significant figures in the life of the Church, from the Apostle John to Gregory the Theologian to Maximos the Confessor to Gregory Palamas.

Integrating dogmatic theology more closely with spirituality and sacramental theology, in turn, would also help to make Western Christian soteriology more explicitly pneumatological. Unfortunately, the pneumatology of the *Joint Declaration* is relatively weak.[95] Spirituality and sacramental theology are only occasionally referenced, with apparently more stress on these areas from the Roman Catholic participants than from the Lutheran.[96] By contrast, the Holy Spirit is crucial to Orthodoxy's ontologically incarnational soteriology, conceived as both restoration and deification. Its dynamic and relational nature, and the emphasis on free human responsiveness to God's initiative, seen especially in the East's consistent integration of its soteriology into its sacramental theology, make it inherently pneumatological. It was through the Holy Spirit that the Son of God became incarnate; it was through the Holy Spirit that Jesus Christ was raised from the dead; it is through the Holy Spirit that we are doubly initiated into the twofold salvific effects of the Incarnation—restoration of our fallen nature through baptism, and the beginning of our growth toward *theosis* through the reception of the Holy Spirit in chrismation; and it is through the Holy Spirit (the *epiclesis* or "calling upon") that communally we are united to Christ, present in the Eucharist.

The criticisms and suggestions in this article should not be interpreted to mean that the *Joint Declaration* is a failure, or, worse yet, useless. The lifting of condemnations over four centuries old, and the recognition of a like theology in two important Churches not in communion, is a cause for rejoicing. And, of course, Orthodoxy agrees with both Roman Catholicism and Lutheranism in the fundamental theme of the *Joint Declaration*: works do not save us, Christ does.

And yet, salvation is an ongoing process of existential faith: as St. Paul says, "work out your own salvation with fear and trembling" (Phil 2:12), which the *Joint Declaration* cites in paragraph 12. And so, we do indeed "work out our own salvation." Orthodox soteriology is synergistic, but not in the perceived Pelagian sense which has resulted in such a pejorative connotation to the word synergy in Protestant thought.[97] We do cooperate, or participate, in our salvation precisely because salvation is *relational*—it is union with God—and relationships are not a one-way street. As human beings created in the image of God, we respond freely to God's love and to his restoration of our fallen human nature. As Kallistos Ware asserts,

> As a Trinity of love, God desired to share his life with created persons made in his image, who would be capable of responding to him freely and willingly in a relationship of love. *Where there is no freedom, there can be no love.*[98]

Additional Reading

Anderson, H. George, T. Austin Murphy, and Joseph A. Burgess, eds. *Justification by Faith*. Minneapolis, Minn.: Augsburg Publishing House, 1985.

Braaten, Carl E. and Robert W. Jenson, eds. *Union with Christ: The New Finnish Interpretation of Luther*. Grand Rapids, Mich.: Wm. B. Eerdmans Publishing Co., 1998.

Bray, G. L. "Justification and the Eastern Orthodox Churches." In David Field, ed., *Here We Stand: Justification by Faith Today*. London: Hodder and Stoughton, 1986, 103–19.

Cavanaugh, William T. "A Joint Declaration? Justification as Theosis in Aquinas and Luther." *The Heythrop Journal* 41:3 (July 2000) 265–80.

Edwards, Henry. "Justification, Sanctification and the Eastern Orthodox Concept of 'Theosis.'" *Consensus: A Canadian Lutheran Journal of Theology* 14:1 (1988) 65–80.

Florovsky, Georges. "The Ascetic Ideal and the New Testament: Reflections on the Critique of the Theology of the Reformation." In Richard S. Haugh, gen. ed., *The Byzantine Ascetic and Spiritual Fathers*, vol. 10 in the Collected Works of Georges Florovsky, trans. Raymond Miller et al. Vaduz, Europa: Büchervertriebsanstalt, 1987.

Meyendorff, John and Robert Tobias, eds. and intro. *Salvation in Christ: A Lutheran-Orthodox Dialogue*. Minneapolis, Minn.: Augsburg, 1992.

Williams, Anna. *The Ground of Union: Deification in Aquinas and Palamas*. New York: Oxford University Press, 1999.

Notes

[1] Robert B. Eno, "Some Patristic Views on the Relationship of Faith and Works in Justification," in *Justification by Faith*, ed. H. George Anderson, T. Austin Murphy and Joseph A. Burgess (Minneapolis, Minn.: Augsburg Publishing House, 1985) 125. Of course, Eno here is assuming an Augustinian—and particularly, a Reformation-based Augustinian—interpretation of Paul's writings on sin and justification to be the correct one. This article challenges that interpretation in light of Eastern Christian thought, although the focus here is more on the fourth through seventh centuries as opposed to the second and third centuries.

[2] Actually, priority of tradition is probably true of all confessions, but less consciously, and is often for traditions of more recent provenance. For example, Lutheran theologian Elisabeth Gräb-Schmidt, implicitly recognizing the novel character of Luther's hermeneutics of justification and of individual interpretation of Scripture, applauds his opening Christianity to "a certain freedom from tradition. Tradition as such was no longer sacrosanct. . . . It opened the possibilities for expansion but also for critique of tradition." Elisabeth Gräb-Schmidt, "The significance of justification in the modern intercultural context. The Papers of Christina Grenholm and Susanne Heine," *LWF Documentation*, no. 45 (March 2000) 97. Nevertheless, the contributors to that issue of the journal, as well as Lutheran theologians in bilateral and ecumenical dialogues, appear to hold the theology of Martin Luther as normatively as Roman Catholics might that of Augustine and Aquinas, and appear absolutely committed to retaining intact the soteriological tradition begun by Luther and the fundamentally forensic understanding of that soteriology which developed in the Lutheran communion.

[3] The Orthodox rejection of *sola scriptura* is even more pronounced when that *scriptura* has been altered to fit a particular interpretation. More specifically, when the Eastern Church reads "justification by faith" in Romans, not only does it reject a legalistic or forensic interpretation of "justification," but it does not infer the word "alone." It is not simply that neither Romans 3:28, Romans 5:1, nor Galatians 3:24 includes the word "alone." More importantly, Orthodox exegesis, when used as the biblical basis of a doctrine, tends to be done intertextually, and there is a strong reliance on how the early Church interpreted a biblical text in context. It is for this reason that Orthodoxy rejects Lutheran soteriology based on the doctrine of justification by faith *alone*: neither the scriptural context nor patristic exegeses of the key passages support such an interpretation. Chrysostom, for instance, in his *Homilies on Romans* clearly understands that Paul is arguing against a Jewish notion of justification through formulaic obedience to the Mosaic Law—he is *not* referring to works of righteousness in the Spirit. See John Chrysostom, *Homilies on the Epistle to the Romans*, Hom. 7, PG 60:441-454; in *NPNF*, First Series, vol. 11. For a modern Orthodox theological critique, see, e.g., Georges Florovsky, "The Ascetic Ideal and the New Testament," 56–58, in Georges Florovsky, "The Ascetic Ideal and the New Testament: Reflections on the Critique of the Theology of the Reformation," trans. Raymond Miller et al., in *Collected Works of Georges Florovsky*, ed. Richard S. Haugh, vol. 10, *Byzantine Ascetic and Spiritual Fathers* (Vaduz, Europa: Büchervertriebsanstalt, 1987). Florovsky criticizes Luther specifically but also, more broadly, he challenges Reformation theologians' definitions of justification for their incongruity with Augustine's actual thought.

[4] William Rusch, referring to both these Western Christian controversies over against Eastern Church history, remarks: "The West also was more legalistic. As the penitential system of the Western Church developed, *justificare* played a role in soteriological thinking that *dikaioo* did not assume in the East. Also the influence of the Pelagian controversy marked the Western Church in ways unknown in the East. . . . [Eastern theologians were] developers of a theology of salvation outside the framework of justi-

fication categories." William G. Rusch, "How the Eastern Fathers Understood What the Western Church Meant by Justification," in *Justification by Faith*, ed. H. George Anderson, T. Austin Murphy and Joseph A. Burgess (Minneapolis: Augsburg Publishing House, 1985) 132–33. Of course, this is precisely because the Eastern Christian understanding of justification was never "forensic" in nature.

[5] Jerome and Orosius might have had more success had they concentrated their criticism on Pelagius and his followers' rather minimalist and nonexistential understanding of both sin and salvation, but Pelagian anthropology regarding free will was far closer to the Christian East's than was Augustine's.

[6] Bibliography on this is, unfortunately, limited. See George Mastrontonis, *Augsburg and Constantinople* (Brookline, Mass.: Holy Cross Orthodox Press, 1982), and Wayne James Jorgenson, "The Augustana Graeca and the Correspondence between the Tübingen Lutherans and Patriarch Jeremias: Scripture and Tradition in Theological Methodology," Ph.D. dissertation, Boston University, 1979.

[7] Rusch, "How the Eastern Fathers," 132.

[8] Augsburg Confession, II, in Theodore G. Tappert, ed., *The Book of Concord* (Philadelphia: Muhlenberg Press, 1959) 29; quoted in Carl A. Volz, "Human Participation in the Divine-Human Dialogue," in *Salvation in Christ: A Lutheran-Orthodox Dialogue*, ed. John Meyendorff and Robert Tobias (Minneapolis: Augsburg, 1992) 86–87.

[9] That is, after the Fall from paradise and grace, as opposed to prelapsarian, or before the Fall.

[10] Volz, "Human Participation," 86.

[11] Ibid., 88.

[12] Interview, *Time*, 21 March 1969, p. 62; quoted in Volz, "Human Participation," 89.

[13] E.g., McBrien, *Catholicism*, vol. 1 (Minneapolis: Winston Press, 1980) 165–67.

[14] It is important to note that the Latin translation Augustine used gave a very different meaning: "and so death spread to all men in whom all have." Inaccurate translations of key passages can have serious consequences; for instance, the translation used by Carl Volz above, for Psalm 51:5 (50:5 LXX)—"Indeed, I was born guilty, a sinner when my mother conceived me"—is notably traducian, unlike the Greek Septuagint text, which uses the plural "sins" and would more accurately be translated as, "Indeed, I was born into transgressions, and into sins did my mother conceive me," thus giving the sense of a sinful human environment rather than of an ontologically sinful, inherited human nature.

[15] Cappadocia is a region in central Asia Minor (modern-day Turkey). The phrase "the Cappadocians" refers to three of the fourth-century's (or any century's) greatest theologians: Basil of Caesarea, called Basil the Great; Gregory of Nazianzus, called Gregory the Theologian; and Gregory of Nyssa, younger brother of Basil.

[16] Rusch, "How the Eastern Fathers," 134.

[17] John Chrysostom, *Homily 10*, PG 60:474; in *NPNF*, First Series, no. 11, p. 401. Augustine's unique interpretation, most scholars believe, was probably due, at least in part, to an inaccurate Latin translation of a key Greek phrase, which is translated by most modern scholars, and traditionally by the Christian East, as "in that [all have sinned]," but which was interpreted in Latin as "in *whom* [all have sinned]," the "whom" referring to Adam. Ross Aden, "Justification and Sanctification: A Conversation Between Lutheranism and Orthodoxy," *St. Vladimir's Theological Quarterly* 38, no. 1 (1994) 94–96. See n.14, above, for another example of how particular translations further particular theological views perhaps not intended in the biblical text.

[18] John Meyendorff provides a short but excellent analysis of Greek patristic exegetical approaches to this key passage from Romans, focusing on Cyril of Alexandria and Theodoret of Cyr, in "Anthropology and Original Sin," *John XXIII Lectures*, vol. 1 (New York: Fordham University Press, 1966) 52–58, esp. 54–56. Meyendorff's recognition of

the existential nature of "corruption" (*phthora*) as a cosmic state in Cyril and of sin as a result of the need for "things" by mortal beings, as understood by Theodoret, contrasts markedly to the legalistic exegeses of Romans 5 common in the Christian West from Augustine on, particularly in Reformation writers.

[19] "Lutherans have not followed Augustine to his unacceptable conclusion that unbaptized infants are condemned. Rather, they emphasize the need for a child to enter the community of grace as soon as possible in order to grow in faith toward God. Baptism was intended for those who will physically and spiritually grow and mature; it was not intended as the last rites." Volz, "Human Participation," 88.

[20] John Chrysostom, *Baptismal Instruction* 3:6, in *Jean Chrysostome: Huit Catéchèses Baptismales Inédites*, ed. and trans. Antoine Wenger, Sources Chrétiennes, vol. 50 (Paris: Éditions du Cerf, 1957) 153–54; English translation in John Chrysostom, *Baptismal Instructions*, trans. Paul W. Harkins, vol. 31 of *Ancient Christian Writers* (Westminster, Md.: Newman Press, 1963) 57.

[21] The roots of this separation of the twofold rites of initiation are practical in nature, that is, the unavailability of the bishop—who always performed baptism *and* chrismation together in the early Church—on a regular basis in each local parish by the medieval period. The Christian East responded to this by allowing presbyters (priests) to celebrate the rites of initiation; the West allowed presbyters (and, later, deacons) to perform baptism but kept the bishop involved as the only celebrant of chrismation. However, the Western Church's ability to conceive of a bifurcation of the rite of initiation, with the result that young children were baptized but not yet fully members of the Church, was predicated on Augustinian theology, I believe.

[22] *The First Answer of Patriarch Jeremiah [II] of Constantinople Concerning the Augsburg Confession*, in Mastrontonis, *Augsburg*, 54.

[23] Gregory of Nyssa, *Sixth Homily on the Beatitudes*, Werner Jaeger, ed., *Gregorii Nysseni Opera*, vol. 7 (Leiden, 1960-) 2:141–44. English translation; trans. Anthony Meredith, *Gregory of Nyssa*, in *The Early Christian Fathers*, ed. Carol Harrison (London: Routledge, 1999) 95–97.

[24] Robert L. Wilken, "The Image of God in Classical Lutheran Theology," in *Salvation in Christ: A Lutheran-Orthodox Dialogue*, ed. John Meyendorff and Robert Tobias (Minneapolis: Augsburg, 1992) 121–32.

[25] Even someone like Gregory of Nyssa, who uses the terms interchangeably, nevertheless clearly articulates a qualitative difference between traits like reason (normally considered part of the "image") and virtue ("likeness").

[26] This interpretation is sometimes positively described as christological since it catalogs what Christ restores to human nature, but it is based on his restoring that which was lost.

[27] Wilken, "The Image of God," 126.

[28] Ibid., 131.

[29] Martin Luther, *Lectures on Genesis* in Jaroslav Pelikan and Helmut T. Lehmann, eds., *Luther's Works*, vol. 1 (St. Louis: Concordia Publishing House and Philadelphia: Fortress Press, 1958) 61; quoted in Wilken, "The Image of God," 126.

[30] "Proinde negare, quod amissa sit imago Dei, est ipsum peccatum originale negare." Wilken, "The Image of God," 131. In the modern context of ecumenical dialogue, at least some Lutheran theologians have questioned their tradition's approach while recognizing its inherent pessimism. For example, Carl Volz opines that "it is incorrect to speak of humanity's 'total depravity' or as human nature being sinful in its essence in the Augustinian sense. Therefore it seems that Luther's idea of losing the image of God entirely cannot be upheld. . . . Nevertheless it can be said that Lutherans espouse a basically pessimistic view of humanity in the sight of God, more so, it appears, than the Orthodox churches, the Roman church, or many Protestant communions." Volz,

"Human Participation," 90. It may be that the classical Lutheran rejection of the historical Christian distinction between image and likeness, and of a positive interpretation of the image as qualities retained in part by postlapsarian human nature, was necessary in order to be consistent with a soteriological emphasis on forensic justification.

[31] Gregory of Nyssa, *De hominis opificio*, PG 44:184B; *On the Making of Man*, XVI, 11, in *NPNF*, Second Series, vol. 5, 405.

[32] John Chrysostom, *Homilies on the Epistle to the Hebrews*, Hom. 12, 5, PG 63:99; in *NPNF*, First Series, vol. 14, 425.

[33] Mastrontonis, *Augsburg*, 83.

[34] Martin Luther, *Ground and Reason of Articles Unjustly Condemned*, WA 7:445; quoted in Volz, "Human Participation," 90. Volz notes that, as opposed to Erasmus, who followed Aquinas, Luther (somewhat) followed Peter Lombard. While humanity has free will in the exercise of matters at the created level, "[f]or Luther, our will is in bondage to all matters pertaining to salvation." Volz, "Human Participation," 91.

[35] Par. 21.

[36] Par. 20.

[37] Par. 19.

[38] It appears that the *Joint Declaration*, while incorporating some of the agreements reached in bilateral dialogues, does not include others. For instance, among the joint work products of the Finnish Lutheran-Russian Orthodox bilateral dialogues is a document drafted in Kiev in 1977 and entitled "Salvation as Justification and Deification"; it includes the following statement: "Grace never does violence to a man's personal will, but exerts its influence through it and with it. Every one has the opportunity to refuse consent to God's will or, by the help of the Holy Spirit, to consent to it." (Hannu Kamppuri, ed., *Dialogue between Neighbours* [Helsinki: Luther-Agricola Gesellschaft, 1986] 76; quoted in Risto Saarinen, "Salvation in the Lutheran-Orthodox Dialogue: A Comparative Perspective," in *Union with Christ: The New Finnish Interpretation of Luther*, ed. Carl F. Braaten and Robert W. Jenson [Grand Rapids, Mich.: Wm. B. Eerdmans Publishing Co., 1998] 169). Risto Saarinen notes that the Finnish theologian Tuomo Mannermaa defended the language as a refutation of the "quietist" view, answering charges by Finnish theologians Fredric Cleve and Karl Christian Felmy, among others, that it was semi-Pelagian. Mannermaa claimed that the Orthodox "are in constant doubt that we conceive the human person as a stone or plant or animal which does not possess any freedom whatsoever. For them, freedom belongs to the constitution of human beings." Saarinen, "Salvation in Dialogue," 170. One understands the validity of Mannermaa's concern given the following quote from Carl Braaten.

[39] Carl E. Braaten, *Principles of Lutheran Theology* (Philadelphia: Fortress Press, 1983) 113; quoted in Michael C. D. McDaniel, "Salvation as Justification and *Theosis*," in *Salvation in Christ: A Lutheran-Orthodox Dialogue*, ed. John Meyendorff and Robert Tobias (Minneapolis: Augsburg, 1992) 77.

[40] This, coupled with the Latin belief in inherited original guilt, led to the development in the Roman Church of the doctrine of the immaculate conception of the Virgin Mary. Eastern Christianity, by contrast, has always venerated her because of her free response to God, an acquiescence to God's will as "part of the common human race issued of the first man (Adam), [she] automatically participates in the fallen status and in the 'spiritual death' introduced by the sin of the first man." Bishop Maximos Aghiorgoussis, "Orthodox Soteriology," in *Salvation in Christ: A Lutheran-Orthodox Dialogue*, ed. John Meyendorff and Robert Tobias (Minneapolis: Augsburg, 1992) 39.

[41] The Lutheran Church-Missouri Synod, not a member of the Lutheran World Federation, was not a signatory to the *Joint Declaration*. For several brief discussions of the biblical basis for and Protestant theological disputes over predestination, an Orthodox response, and the Greek and Latin patristic background, see Frederick R. Harm, "Election:

A Lutheran-Biblical View," in *Salvation in Christ: A Lutheran-Orthodox Dialogue*, ed. John Meyendorff and Robert Tobias (Minneapolis: Augsburg, 1992) 133–50; John Breck, "The New Testament Concept of Election," ibid., 151–58; and James Jorgenson, "Predestination According to Divine Foreknowledge in Patristic Tradition," ibid., 159–69. The Roman Church ultimately rejected the full implications of Augustinianism at the Second Council of Orange in 529 ("We do not believe that some are predestined to evil by the divine power"), but maintained prevenient grace (". . . faith . . . was not a gift of nature but a gift of God's generosity.") Jorgenson, "Predestination," 164.

   [42] Section 3, par. 16.

   [43] An excellent overview of Maximos' theology is provided in Andrew Louth, *Maximos the Confessor* (London/New York: Routledge, 1996); see especially 59–62. Theological views of evil as "parasitic" are essentially based on the combination of natural and gnomic will; i.e., the person desires to feel good and complete, but does things which may hurt himself and/or others in a misbegotten effort to fulfill this innate desire.

   [44] Maximos then applied this theological anthropology to the unique situation of the *theanthropos*—the God-Man, Jesus Christ. Christ has a natural human will, oriented toward God, but not a gnomic will. This is because the gnomic will is a personal attribute. The asymmetric Christology of the Third and Fifth Ecumenical Councils, applied to the question of personal will, leads inevitably to the recognition that the personal will of Christ is the divine will. Therefore, in the person of Jesus Christ, his natural human will fulfills its inclination toward God and therefore can only be distinguished in theory from his divine will, and from the fact that the human process of deliberation is occasionally evident (e.g., in the Garden of Gethsemani) in the form of conscious conformation to the divine will, but not in the sense of an inability to discern the divine will or, even worse, a willing rejection of it.

   [45] Rusch, "How the Eastern Fathers," 141.

   [46] Louth, *Maximos*, 61.

   [47] Ibid., 61.

   [48] Eric W. Gritsch and Robert W. Jenson, *Lutheranism: The Theological Movement and Its Confessional Writings* (Philadelphia: Fortress Press, 1976) 36; quoted in McDaniel, "Salvation," 69.

   [49] See the quote from William Rusch, n. 4, above.

   [50] As the Lutheran theologian Carl Braaten has asserted: "The whole of theology is inherently developed from a soteriological point of view. Salvation is not one of the main topics, along with the doctrine of God, Christ, church. . . . It is rather the perspective from which all these subjects are interpreted." Carl E. Braaten, *Principles of Lutheran Theology* (Philadelphia: Fortress Press, 1963) 63; quoted in McDaniel, "Salvation," 67.

   [51] Bernhard Lohse, *A Short History of Christian Doctrine*, trans. F. Ernest Stoeffler (Philadelphia: Fortress Press, 1966) 169; quoted in McDaniel, "Salvation," 69.

   [52] This fact, plus the lack of a soteriology based on atonement or justification, explains why in the Christian East the Cross—while extremely important soteriologically—has never had the segregated, unique soteriological role it plays in Western Christianity.

   [53] Lutheran theologians would likely disagree with this description. For instance, one of the sources listed for 4.2 of the *Joint Declaration* asserts: "By justification we are both declared and made righteous. Justification, therefore, is not a legal fiction. God, in justifying, effects what he promises; he forgives sin and makes us truly righteous." (Justification by Faith" in *Lutherans and Catholics in Dialogue*, VII [Minneapolis: Augsburg Publishing House, 1985] sec. 156, 5; p. 71). However, the notion repeatedly stated in Lutheran writings that the justified person is *simul justus et peccator* ("simultaneously righteous and a sinner") can only be understood in a juridical sense since it is ontologically incomprehensible. As one puzzled Orthodox theologian has remarked, "People in

communion with Christ's humanity, 'conformed to the image of Christ,' cannot be 'sinful and righteous' at the same time, with a mere 'imputed' righteousness. . . . Once justified, people are also sanctified by the life of Christ in the Holy Spirit." Aghiorgoussis, "Orthodox Soteriology," 49.

[54] Gregory of Nyssa, *Against Eunomius*, 2.91; quoted in Aghiorgoussis, "Orthodox Soteriology," 49.

[55] The Second Ecumenical Council, Constantinople I, held in 381, dealt with Arianism and also with Apollinarianism, which denied that Christ possessed a rational soul; the Fourth Ecumenical Council, held in Chalcedon in 451, rejected "Monophysitism" ("one nature" in Christ), affirming that Jesus Christ exists "in two natures" and is completely human, i.e., he assumed a human nature exactly like ours in everything "except sin"; the Sixth Ecumenical Council was discussed earlier; the Seventh Ecumenical Council, Nicaea II, convoked in 787, declared that Jesus Christ can and must be depicted in images (icons) because of his truly human incarnation.

[56] Gregory of Nazianzus, *Letter 101* (*To Cledonius*), 32, PG 37:181C-184A; in *NPNF*, Second Series, vol. 7, 440.

[57] Kallistos Ware, *The Orthodox Way*, rev. ed. (Crestwood, N.Y.: St. Vladimir's Seminary Press, 1995) 73–76.

[58] Lucian Turcescu, "Soteriological Issues in the Joint Declaration: An Orthodox Perspective," paper presented at the Annual Meeting of the North American Academy of Ecumenists, September 28–30, Eckerd College, St. Petersburg, Fla., 2001.

[59] See, e.g., Aden, "Justification and Sanctification."

[60] See, e.g., John Chrysostom, *Homily 10 on Romans*, PG 60:473-80; English translation in *NPNF*, First Series, vol. 11, 401–05. Chrysostom is adamant that, just as Adam's sin led to death to all humanity, so Christ's death and resurrection have led to the justification of all humanity.

[61] Lutheran theologian Susanne Heine has advocated a clearer recognition of the ontological significance of the doctrine of justification by faith, and finds [Western] Christianity at a disadvantage to Eastern religions whose theologies are based on an ontological interrelationality of all things. See Susanne Heine, "Being precedes doing. The ontological approach to justification with reference to interreligious dialogue," *LWF Documentation*, no. 45 (March 2000) 81–93.

[62] John Breck, "Divine Initiative: Salvation in Orthodox Theology," in *Salvation in Christ: A Lutheran-Orthodox Dialogue*, ed. John Meyendorff and Robert Tobias (Minneapolis: Augsburg, 1992) 116.

[63] John Meyendorff, *Byzantine Theology* (New York: Fordham University Press, 1974) 160–01; quoted in Aghiorgoussis, "Orthodox Soteriology," 46.

[64] There are relatively few Greek patristic references to a juridical soteriology; perhaps the most notable is Athanasius in *De incarnatione* 20:2: "But since the debt owed by all men had still to be paid, since all . . . had to die, therefore after the proof of his divinity given by his works, he now on behalf of all men offered the sacrifice and surrendered his own temple to death on behalf of all, in order to make them all guiltless and free from the first transgression, and to reveal himself superior to death, showing his own incorruptible body as first-fruits of the universal resurrection." Athanasius, *Contra gentes* and *De incarnatione*, ed. Robert W. Thomson (Oxford: Clarendon Press, 1971) 183; reprinted in "Common Statement: Christ 'in Us' and Christ 'for Us' in Lutheran and Orthodox Theology," in *Salvation in Christ: A Lutheran-Orthodox Dialogue*, ed. John Meyendorff and Robert Tobias (Minneapolis: Augsburg, 1992) 24. However, for Athanasius, as for other Eastern Christian writers, the focus is on overcoming death through Christ's consubstantial unity with humanity, which heals human nature, and restores its capacity for deification. E.g., earlier in *De incarnatione*, Athanasius moves seamlessly from "debt" language to "union" and "nature" language: "For being over all, the Word of God naturally

by offering His own temple and corporeal instrument for the life of all satisfied the debt by His death. And thus He, the incorruptible Son of God, being conjoined with all by a like nature, naturally clothed all with incorruption, by the promise of the resurrection." *On the Incarnation*, 9, 2, in *NPNF*, Second Series, vol. 4, 41.

[65] "Common Statement," 25.

[66] The broader consequences are evident in Paul, e.g., in Romans 8, in Irenaeus's theology of recapitulation, and in Maximos the Confessor's theology of humanity's overcoming the divisions within all parts of creation. Even John Chrysostom, the Greek Father perhaps most beloved by Western, especially evangelical, Christians, describes Christ's death and resurrection as having universal and even cosmic significance—contrast, e.g., Chrysostom's exegesis of Romans 5 (PG 60:474-480) with that of Augustine or Luther. As John Meyendorff declares, "The Christ-event is a cosmic event both because Christ is the Logos—and, therefore, in God the agent of creation—and because He is man, since man is a 'microcosm.' Man's sin plunges creation into death and decay, but man's restoration in Christ is a restoration of the cosmos to its original beauty." John Meyendorff, *Byzantine Theology* (New York: Fordham University Press, 1974) 152; quoted in Aghiorgoussis, "Orthodox Soteriology," 43.

[67] Breck, "Divine Initiative," 108–09.

[68] Rusch, "How the Eastern Fathers," 134.

[69] John Meyendorff, "Humanity: 'Old' and 'New'—Anthropological Considerations," in *Salvation in Christ: A Lutheran-Orthodox Dialogue*, ed. John Meyendorff and Robert Tobias (Minneapolis: Augsburg, 1992) 63.

[70] Ibid., 62.

[71] The biblical *locus classicus* for the doctrine of deification is 2 Peter 1:4, which promises that, through God's power, we may escape from corruption "and may become participants of the divine nature."

[72] Athanasius, *On the Incarnation* 54; PG 25:192B; in *NPNF*, Second Series, vol. 4, 65.

[73] Athanasius, *Defense of the Nicene Definition*, 3, 14, PG 25:448C-448D; in *NPNF*, Second Series, vol. 4, 159.

[74] Rusch, "How the Eastern Fathers," 136–40.

[75] See, e.g., *Against the Heresies*, 5, 1, 1.

[76] *The Teacher (Paedagogus)*, 1, 5, 26; *Miscellanies (Stromata)*, 5, 10, 63, etc.

[77] *On Prayer (De oratione)*, 27, 13; *Commentary on John* 29, 27, 29.

[78] Breck, "Divine Initiative," 116.

[79] Rusch, "How the Eastern Fathers," 136.

[80] Maximos the Confessor, *De ambigua* 41, PG 91:1308D, in Louth, *Maximos*, 159.

[81] A number of women mystics from various Western European cultures use particularly strong imagery for this union, e.g., Hildegard of Bingen, Teresa of Avila, and Julian of Norwich.

[82] "In Aquinas's realist epistemology, knowledge is a form of participation, since to know something is to become conformed to it, to possess its form without actually being it. To understand a nature is to receive the form of that nature in the mind immaterially." William T. Cavanaugh, "A Joint Declaration? Justification as Theosis in Aquinas and Luther," *The Heythrop Journal* 41, no. 3 (third quarter 2000) 272–73.

[83] Cavanaugh, "A Joint Declaration?," 279. In fact, for Aquinas, the only grace which is truly uncreated is the grace of the inner life of the Trinity (i.e., the immanent Trinity), in which created beings cannot participate.

[84] E.g., Karl Rahner, *Nature and Grace: Dilemmas in the Modern Church*, trans. Dinah Wharton (London: Burns and Oates/New York: Sheed and Ward, 1964). For an overall analysis of nature and grace in such theologians as de Lubac, Rahner, and von Balthasar, see Stephen J. Duffy, *The Graced Horizon: Nature and Grace in Modern Catholic Thought*, Theology and Life Series, vol. 37 (Collegeville, Minn.: Michael Glazier/The Liturgical Press, 1992).

[85] See, e.g., Gregory Palamas, *The Triads*, ed. John Meyendorff, trans. Nicholas Gendle (New York: Paulist Press, 1983).

[86] The English title of Orthodox theologian Panayiotis Nellas' book, *Deification in Christ*, trans. Norman Russell, foreword Bishop Kallistos of Diokleia (Crestwood, New York: St. Vladimir's Seminary Press, 1987), does not capture the full sense of its original Greek title, *Zoon Theouvmenon*, which might more literally be translated as "Deified Animal" or "Deified Creature."

[87] Examples of the research and findings of these Finnish theologians have been brought together in Carl E. Braaten and Robert W. Jenson, eds., *Union with Christ: The New Finnish Interpretation of Luther* (Grand Rapids, Mich.: Wm. B. Eerdmans Publishing Co., 1998).

[88] Tuomo Mannermaa, "Justification and *Theosis* in Lutheran-Orthodox Perspective," in Carl E. Braaten and Robert W. Jenson, eds., *Union with Christ*, 38; the nested quote is from Martin Luther, *Lectures on Galatians*, 1535, Luther, *LW*, vol. 26, 100–30.

[89] Simo Peura, "Christ as Favor and Gift: The Challenge of Luther's Understanding of Justification," in Carl E. Braaten and Robert W. Jenson, eds., *Union with Christ*, 48.

[90] Mannermaa, "Justification and *theosis*," 27–28.

[91] Peura, "Christ as Favor and Gift," 45.

[92] Of course, it seems puzzling that Lutheran theology could have developed so differently from the theology of Luther himself, particularly since Lutheran theologians claim to adhere closely to Luther's own views. Carl Braaten, in his response to Peura's article, notes that "Melanchthon's forensic view of justification prevailed over Osiander's view of the essential indwelling of the righteousness of Christ in the believer." Carl E. Braaten, "Response to Simo Peura, 'Christ as Favor and Gift,'" in Carl E. Braaten and Robert W. Jenson, eds., *Union with Christ*, 73. Equally (if not perhaps more) importantly, Mannermaa summarizes the results of Risto Saarinen's 1989 dissertation, "The Transcendental Interpretation of the Presence-of-Christ Motif in Luther Research," which examines the interpretations by modern scholars of Luther's emphasis on the ontological "presence(Being)-of-Christ" in faith, and details how "the philosophical assumptions of traditional Luther research . . . made it impossible to view Luther's doctrine of justification as a doctrine of real participation or divinization." Tuomo Mannermaa, "Why is Luther So Fascinating? Modern Finnish Luther Research," in Carl E. Braaten and Robert W. Jenson, eds., *Union with Christ*, 3.

[93] Section 4.3 ("Justification by Faith and through Grace"), par. 26, appears to be influenced by the new wave of Finnish Lutheran theology. It relates faith to living in communion with God, and sounds a more organic note. "Because God's act is a new creation, it affects all dimensions of the person and leads to a life in hope and love. In the doctrine of 'justification by faith alone,' a distinction but not a separation is made between justification itself and the renewal of one's way of life that necessarily follows from justification and without which faith does not exist. . . . Justification and renewal are joined in Christ, who is present in faith."

[94] This is not to say that everyone else has moved with the Finnish theologians. For example, Michael McDaniel complains: "To confuse works with faith, law with gospel, or sanctification with justification is to make all the promises of God concerning the forgiveness of sin and everlasting life unintelligible and uncertain." McDaniel, "Salvation," 78. Naturally, the Christian East would disagree.

[95] Paragraphs 15 and 16 of section 3, "The Common Understanding of Justification," recognize the role of the Holy Spirit, but, curiously, the Spirit is almost entirely absent from the explication which follows in section 4.

[96] E.g., paragraphs 24 and 28 in sections 4.2 and 4.4, respectively.

[97] The fear of appearing to allow a role to humanity in justification/salvation is particularly strong in section 4.1, paragraphs 19–21, of the *Joint Declaration*.

[98] Ware, *The Orthodox Way*, 58.

Chapter 9

Justification and the Spirit of Life: A Pentecostal Response to the *Joint Declaration*

_____ *Frank D. Macchia*

I approach the *Joint Declaration on the Doctrine of Justification* as an outsider to the formation of the document, the decades of ecumenical discussion that led to its formation and, to an extent, even the issues that are negotiated in it. Justification by grace through faith has not at all been present as a strong topic in Pentecostal literature, not even in the Wesleyan/Holiness roots from which the Pentecostal movement sprang. But as a Christian, I am connected deeply to the issues addressed in this declaration, and, as a theologian, intensely interested in how such a joint statement can direct us in the future in terms of our confessions, ecumenical discussions, theological reflections, and social praxis. Consequently, I will affirm much of what I find in this significant document. But as an outsider, I will attempt to question the document at a few decisive places in order to urge further discussion of salient issues.

Justification and Deliverance: A Preliminary Reflection

Justification was not part of the language of faith common in the Pentecostal Churches familiar to me in my childhood and youth. We used terms like "born again," "saved by the Blood of the Lamb," or "set free by the glorious Gospel" in order to describe God's act of saving sinners. Our understanding of the "full Gospel," as we termed it, did revolve around the Person of Jesus Christ but was focused on the work of Christ through the agency of the Holy Spirit to deliver us from the power of sin, sickness, and death, and to inspire in us the active faith necessary to please God. I recall a certain "material" notion of salvation among Pentecostals.[1] Divine healing of the body and deliverance from such social conditions as drug addiction or poverty were considered part of the victory of the Cross and the Resurrection over the power of sin in the world. Walter Hollenweger accurately describes the common Pentecostal understanding of salvation through the lens of a Chilean Pentecostal testimony:

> He is now no longer at the mercy of uncertainty, hunger, unemployment, drunkenness, boredom and homelessness, because he has once again become part of a "family", because he has "brothers" and "sisters" who help him and give his life moral direction. They may not teach him to write, but they teach him to read and underline the important passages of the Bible for him. He learns to read not only the Bible, but the newspapers as well, and sends his children to school. And because he no longer throws his money away, he may be able to send one of his sons to study at the university. All of this he owes to the Saviour who has rolled away the burden of his sin, who has led him out of the prison of sin, indifference and hopelessness, and to the Holy Spirit, who has not just to be believed in, but who one can experience in all sorts of marvelous healings.[2]

Christ is said by Pentecostals to save us "fully" through the agency of the Spirit by sanctifying us, healing our bodies, delivering us from the oppression of sin, and coming again one day soon to raise us from the dead or to transform those of us who happen to be alive on earth so that this mortality may put on immortality.

It was not until I entered college that I first heard of the doctrine of justification by grace through faith. I read about it there in Evangelical textbooks and heard about it from professors trained at Baptist or Reformed seminaries. Unfortunately, the doctrine which reached me through these books and lectures highlighted the forensic nature of justification. The metaphor was explained as follows: God, as an impartial judge, had no other choice but to condemn all of us as sinners. But we could have Christ's merited righteousness reckoned to us through faith in him, thus winning God's acquittal. We who trust in the Gospel live each day by God's declaration that we are righteous because of Christ.

I must admit that I was enlightened and grasped by this "new" doctrine. But I was made to wonder: if this doctrine of forensic justification by grace through faith was so central to the Gospel, why had I not heard it before? I began to think that the members of the Pentecostal Churches with which I was familiar needed to be enlightened theologically, and I was determined to enlighten them.

But the disparity between this forensic understanding of justification and the Gospel as I had learned it from my Pentecostal heritage was too great to be ignored for long. In time, questions began to gnaw at me. Where was the work of the Holy Spirit in this doctrine of forensic justification? Where was the centrality of healing? Where was the eschatological horizon and the importance of the Resurrection? Where was the integral relationship of this justification doctrine to sanctification and new life? Where was the stress on my active response of faith to the Word and the Spirit of God and on the pleasure that God takes in such responses? The impartial judge of forensic justification who justifies us due to Christ's merited righteousness lacked connection to the biblical stories that nourished me in the faith. This God of legal justification was distant and lifeless and paled in comparison to the God of the Gospel about whom I had learned earlier, a God who pursues humanity through the Spirit-empowered mission of the Church and provides foretastes of the coming resurrection by breaking the bonds of sin and making people whole both spiritually and physically.

When I first read Trent's description of justification, my heart was "strangely warmed." There in those decrees and councils was an understanding of justification that involved the Spirit's work in sanctification and my active faith response to God. Of course, Trent bothered me as well. The Aristotelian list of causes used to explain the nature and effects of God's justifying grace seemed to my mind to eclipse the Pentecostal focus on the miraculous work of the Spirit in unmediated encounter with the believer in imparting new life, and I missed in these documents what I had valued most about the forensic model of justification, namely, the declaration of God's favor that is heard in the Gospel and that comforts us in weakness and sin.

Of course, I have also learned that the doctrine of justification in both Augustine and Luther was more complex than the forensic model I had learned in college. It was Gustaf Aulén's *Christus Victor*,[3] and the Finnish interpretation of Luther[4] which, in different ways, helped me to gain a new appreciation for Luther's understanding of justification. I can identify with Geoffrey Wainwright's recent statement concerning the possible appeal of Methodists to the "Catholic" Luther.[5] I was initially surprised upon first reading the *Joint Declaration* that such newer readings of Luther were not more thoroughly utilized in connecting with Catholic concerns.

Helpful for me as well was Hans Küng's 1957 dissertation on Barth's doctrine of justification, which gave impetus among many to the possibility that a righteousness declared in the Gospel and embraced in faith can (and must) be linked inseparably with renewal of life. After all, as Küng noted, what God declares is brought to pass, because it is *God's* Word that declares it.[6] Küng was convinced that the difference between Barth and Trent was largely a difference of emphasis and terminology.[7] I find this insight at the heartthrob of the *Joint Declaration*. In justification, "we are accepted by God and receive the Holy Spirit, who renews our hearts" (no. 15). Similarly, Catholics and Lutherans confess that forgiveness of sins "at the same time frees human beings from sin's enslaving power and imparts the gift of new life in Christ" and these actions "are not to be separated" (no. 22). It is noteworthy that the international Catholic-Methodist dialogue as well, while not rejecting forensic categories, claiming that believers are "regarded and treated as righteous," also maintained that this treatment culminates in their participation in the divine.[8]

As significant as this linkage between declared and transforming righteousness is ecumenically in negotiating Protestant and Catholic tensions in justification, they require further elaboration even within the limited confines of a joint declaration. In particular, what is needed is greater clarity concerning the precise theological linkage between the Lutheran emphasis on declared righteousness and the Catholic stress on justification in the renewal of life. It is to this concern that we now turn.

Toward a Pneumatological Foundation for Justification

The *Joint Declaration* affirms that justification is the "work of the Triune God" (no. 15). If justification is accomplished by God as Trinity, it must be both christologically and pneumatologically based. Yet, the explanation of this trinitarian work in the *Joint Declaration* seems to lack a pneumatological foundation, limiting the work of the Spirit to our personal connection to Christ by faith and the fruit of love. This connection is vital for the *Joint Declaration*, since Christ himself is our righteousness: "Christ himself is our righteousness in which we share through the Holy Spirit" (no. 22). In connecting us to Christ, the Spirit is understood to give rise to the personal renewal that comes through faith: "we are accepted by God and receive the Holy Spirit who renews our hearts" (no. 15). In other words, pneumatology is ushered in to explain the dynamics of faith in Christ and the fruit of love, but is absent when describing the very foundation and nature of the righteousness won by Christ in his life, death, and resurrection. Since what little is said in the *Joint Declaration* on the Spirit's work is confined to the personal and ecclesial dynamics of our response to God, it is not clear whether justification has any eschatological or cosmic significance. The Spirit renews our hearts (no. 15), a renewal that is brought to completion in "eternal life" (no. 16). This focus on personal renewal and eternal life is found in certain Pietistic and Evangelical streams of Protestant Church life, except for the ecclesiological/sacramental context for the understanding of justification in the *Joint Declaration*. Such a pneumatological focus on personal renewal, though valuable, is hardly adequate for a joint Lutheran and Catholic declaration that is fully responsive to contemporary theological developments in both traditions.

There are hints in a few places that the text wants to break out of the confines of the individualistic and ecclesiological focus on the Spirit. Justification is said to affect "all dimensions of the person" and lead to "a life in hope" because "God's act is a new creation" (no. 26). But the implication here is that God's creative act is to be understood within the narrow confines of the granting of faith "by his creative word" (Ibid.). In justification, we are united with Christ's death and resurrection (no. 11) and receive both "justification and life" (no. 12). But every indication is that, if the Spirit is involved in this connection between justification and new life, such involvement is limited to the personal appropriation of Christ's righteousness in faith, hope, and love. Again, though such a pneumatological focus has value, it is inadequate as a context in which the ecumenical possibilities of justification are affirmed.

This personal and ecclesial focus on pneumatology must be affirmed but does not proceed far enough. Left unstated in the *Joint Declaration* is the vital role of the Spirit in Christ's foundational act of establishing righteousness through his life, death, and resurrection. I wish to maintain that such a pneumatological foundation in the Christ event would reach beyond Christ's resurrection toward an understanding of the fulfillment of all righteousness that involves the very renewal of creation. There has been a renewed awareness recently of the significance of Spirit Christology for overcoming the atrophied pneumatology of the West that restricts the Spirit's work to the realization of new life in faith and love.[9] The awareness of the foundational role of the Spirit in the inauguration of righteousness in the work of

Christ is needed in the *Joint Declaration* if the full eschatological, cosmic, and, even social implications of justification are to be appreciated and shared ecumenically.

Noting the absence of this foundational role for the Spirit in justification is not an exercise in theological hairsplitting. This point has serious implications for how the declaration understands the very nature of the righteousness to which we lay claim in faith and which changes us even now in significant ways. The absence of a foundational role for the Spirit in justification leads, therefore, to a fundamental ambiguity in the declaration as to whether or not there is any basis for connecting declared righteousness and renewal of life other than the subjective experience of the saving presence of Christ through Word and sacrament. We are left to wonder what the nature of the righteousness *is* that Christ has won for us, how it is that he has won it, and the direction and breadth of this righteousness in the world.

The term "righteousness" is used extensively in paragraphs 8 to 10 but without much definition, either christologically or pneumatologically. The closest one comes to a definition is the statement that for Paul righteousness is "also God's power for those who have faith" (no. 10). This power becomes ours through faith. What follows, however, is not a pneumatological explanation as to why Christ's righteousness is power and toward what end this power is directed. Instead, what follows is a sacrificial understanding of the atonement which becomes "effective through faith" (Ibid.). Again, it is the experience of our response to God in the Church that becomes the context for explaining the realm of power and renewal. If the declaration is to be truly trinitarian, a clear understanding of the Spirit's contribution is needed beyond the confines of our corporate and individual life of faith and love. It is to this point that we turn next.

The Spirit of Life and the Righteousness of the Kingdom of God

I want to suggest that the righteousness which justifies us, if both christologically and pneumatologically defined, will involve a great deal more than merited favor with God and forgiveness. It will involve deliverance from sin, injustice, and oppression, as well as the inauguration of new creation (my Pentecostal colors are showing). In other words, it will involve the righteousness of the kingdom of God which is both cosmic and eschatological in significance. If one ignores such a foundational role for the Spirit and confines the work of the Spirit to the reception of Christ's work in faith, the tendency will be to view the Spirit's work individualistically (at most, ecclesiologically). As noted above, it is not surprising that the *Joint Declaration* views the renewal of life as the renewal of our hearts (no. 15) which is completed in eternal life (no. 16). The cosmic implications of justification are absent from the *Joint Declaration*.

It was during my dissertation work in the theology of the turn-of-the-century German Pietist, Christoph Blumhardt, that my attention concerning justification was directed beyond the confines of the life of personal faith and love to the burning issue of the kingdom of God on earth. Christoph Blumhardt took his father's healing ministry in the direction of social activism as a socialist politician. His "turn to the world" had a seminal influence on the young Karl Barth, as well as on Paul Tillich, Dietrich Bonhoeffer, and Jürgen Moltmann.[10] I recall being stunned by Blumhardt's statement in the midst of his focus on the kingdom of God that the doctrine of justification was "meaningless to the One whose mighty hand sets us free."[11] I had already begun to wonder whether the doctrine of justification held any promise for Pentecostal theology. Were we to dismiss it as an incidental Pauline polemic?

Later, I read an article by Jürgen Moltmann entitled, "What Does the Term 'Evangelical' Mean Today?" (*Was heisst heute 'evangelisch'?*). It was interestingly subtitled, "From the Doctrine of Justification to the Theology of the Kingdom of God" (*Von der Rechtfertigungslehre zur Reich-Gottes-Theologie*).[12] In this article, Moltmann traces the influence of Christoph Blumhardt and Leonard Ragaz on broadening the center of his Evangelical identity from justification by faith to the more-encompassing hope for the coming kingdom of God in righteousness and justice. He criticizes a doctrine of justification that is based solely on the Cross and involved merely with the forgiveness of sins. For Moltmann, Christ is viewed as the locus for the accomplishment of such kingdom righteousness by the Spirit of new life. Here in seminal form was an understanding of justification that resonated with the Pentecostal understanding of salvation that has shaped my understanding of the Gospel in decisive ways.

As I have implied above, the *Joint Declaration* seems to reach out for such a definition but does not quite grasp it. My thoughts on the liberating and transforming nature of righteousness as the work of the Spirit are inspired in part by the work of certain biblical scholars who have pointed to the fact that righteousness and justice in the Scriptures are concepts of vast cosmic and eschatological significance. Brevard

Childs, for example, claims that in the Old Testament "righteousness" reaches to all of creation, to a "cosmic order" that spans law, wisdom, nature, and politics. The cosmic goal of righteousness suggests an eschatological dimension to justification. Childs notes that in the late postexilic and Hellenistic periods, "the eschatological longing for the manifestation of God's righteous salvation increases in predominance."[13] Hans Heinrich Schmid could even state that, in the Old Testament, the "establishment of justice and righteousness is nothing less than a creation event."[14]

The sense of forensic judgment is not absent in the Old Testament. God declares in advance what God will do and these words sustain people in faith, even in absence of sight (Isa 46:10). And, as Thomas Finger notes rightly, the legal implications of forensic justification in the Old Testament are highly metaphorical. He points out that God's forensic judgment takes place in the midst of "clashes among political and cosmic forces and of God's righteousness as a power which overcomes them in concrete reality."[15]

Käsemann finds the same understanding of forensic justification in Paul. As Käsemann has noted, the Old Testament and Jewish apocalyptic backgrounds inform Paul's reference to the saving righteousness of God as both a gift and the redemptive power by which God manifests God's eschatological saving activity toward creation. According to Käsemann, Paul was convinced that justification would be achieved through Christ's death and resurrection, which set in motion an "eschatological hope of a cosmic restoration" that "has already appeared as a present reality to be grasped in faith."[16] It seems to me that this direction for a theology of justification complements the focus of the Finnish interpretation of Luther on our participation in Christ by granting it a more robust eschatological and cosmic fulfillment.

Christ's work in fulfilling all righteousness as the person of the Spirit fulfills the Old Testament and ancient Jewish understanding of the righteousness of God. My own effort to work out the implications of a Spirit Christology for understanding the role of Christ as the justified man began with a discovery of the significance of Romans 4:25.[17] This text reads that Christ was "put to death for our transgressions but raised for our justification." The fact that this Pauline text makes the foundation of justification the decisive act of new creation by the Spirit of God, namely, the resurrection of Christ, was extremely intriguing for me. Theology in the West has been influenced by a loss of emphasis on the significance of the Spirit for Jesus' role as Redeemer. Note in particular the tendency in Protestant theology, including Wesley, to confine justification to the Cross as the event in which God's justice and wrath were satisfied and the basis of justification of the sinner established. Since the New Testament witness clearly established the resurrection of Christ as an event of the Spirit (Rom 8:11), the Resurrection was thus reserved for the basis of our subjective faith response to a justification "objectively" won in the Cross. It is then sanctification that has its basis in the Resurrection. The Cross justifies by satisfying God's justice while the Resurrection sanctifies with new life. The end result is that the Spirit has nothing directly to do with the origin or foundation of justification.

Joseph Fitzmeyer thus complains that the Resurrection as an event of the Spirit was viewed as "an appendage or even as an exemplary confirmation of Jesus' death, which was considered to be the real cause of forgiveness of sins and justification."[18] If the Cross and not the Resurrection is the real basis for justification, what is one to do with Romans 4:25 which states that Christ was "raised for our justification?" There are commentators who have gone out of their way to avoid the implication that Romans 4:25, especially in the light of 8:11, clearly makes Jesus' resurrection by the Spirit of God the very basis of our justification. For example, Charles Hodge states that Romans 4:25 regards the resurrection as the mere "evidence" that justification through the satisfaction of the Cross has been accomplished.[19] In what almost seems to be a protest against this text, Everett Harrison in his commentary on Romans states, "It may be helpful to recognize that justification, considered objectively from the standpoint of God's provision, was indeed accomplished in the death of Christ and therefore did not require the resurrection to complete it."[20]

Romans 4:25 suggests, however, that justification may be viewed as accomplished by the Spirit in the resurrection of Jesus and, ultimately, in our resurrection and the coming new heavens and new earth. Justice and righteousness are accomplished through the new-creation work of the Spirit as God fulfills the divine covenant obligations to creation and delivers creation from the injustice of bondage to sin and death. In justification through new creation, the victims of injustice are delivered and grace is offered to the perpetrators of injustice who require deliverance as well.

The justice accomplished by Christ, as Moltmann noted, was not "works centered" (i.e., merited righteousness) but "victim centered" (the deliverance from oppression and death).[21] It is accomplished in the deliverance of creation from sin, oppression, and death. Paul's entire insistence is that justification does not come through the Law but through God's saving act in Christ and the Spirit, which is experienced as a foretaste now through the gift of the Spirit and is culminated in the resurrection of the body and the new creation. Paul assumes, for example in Romans, chapters 7 and 8, that new creation through Christ and the Spirit and not the Law represents the locus of God's saving righteousness, for "what the law could not do, God did by sending God's Son into the world" (Rom 8:3). The Law is "holy, just, and good" (Rom 7:12) but it is not the means by which God's new life in the Spirit is realized. The entire thrust of Paul's statements about the impotence of the works of law to justify in Romans 7 is meant to lead the reader to the conclusion that the new life of the Spirit depicted in chapter 8 comes only through Christ's death and resurrection by the Spirit of God, for "if the Spirit of him who raised Jesus from the dead dwells in you, he who raised Christ from the dead will give life to your mortal bodies also through his Spirit who dwells in you" (8:11).

It is not that in Paul's mind some abstract notion of divine justice cannot be satisfied or merited among us by the works of the Law with the result that Christ had to merit it for us. No, this is not the point for Paul. Rather, the point is that the Spirit and not the Law brings the new life that will be fulfilled in the achievement of final justice through new creation. The presence of the living Christ through the Spirit among us allows us to experience this justified new creation as belonging to us already in faith. The importance of the Spirit as the means of bringing about final righteousness in new creation is the reason why faith and not the works of the Law is the means by which this new creation lays claim to us in the here and now. We walk by faith and not by sight. In Galatians, one can also find this theme of justification as new creation grasped presently through the gift of the Spirit received in faith. For Paul in Galatians, the "blessing of Abraham" is designated as both justification and the gift of the Spirit as the foretaste of new creation to come (chs. 2–3).

Righteousness is "reckoned" to us in faith (Rom 4:23), not because Christ's "merits" have been transferred to us, but rather because the future new creation to be experienced in the resurrection has already laid claim to us in our present state through the presence of the Spirit and our corresponding response of faith, as well as hope and love. Paul, therefore, states in the very next verse, 4:24, that righteousness will be reckoned to us who believe "in him who raised Jesus from the dead," and then follows in 4:25 with the words that Christ "was put to death for our trespasses and raised for our justification." In other words, the righteousness that is reckoned to us in faith is not defined as meritorious works transferred to us from Christ but instead as the new life of the Spirit unleashed in the Resurrection and yet to be fulfilled in new creation. Justification is a gift given by grace alone, and received by faith, because it comes to us as a work of the Spirit through Christ. As the new-creation work of the Spirit it cannot be earned or even received through our acts of piety.

As the man of the Spirit, Jesus proclaims the year of the Lord's favor and then defines this favor as the liberation of the oppressed, God's redemptive justice in action (Luke 4:18f.). In his death and resurrection, God's redemptive justice is fulfilled by the Spirit of new life. Jesus is raised as the new creation, the man of the Spirit, the justified man. If justification is achieved by the Spirit in Christ through the resurrection of an oppressed and murdered Jew who gave his life for redemption and reconciliation, then justification has profound implications for ethics today. In a graceless world plagued by death and destruction, the just creation accomplished in Christ by the Spirit explodes with new possibilities for life. In an increasingly graceless world in which people are denied many essential qualities of life because of their race, sex, age, physical stature, or social class, justification by the gracious acts of God through the Spirit in Christ as the new creation implies constant protest and confrontation. There is no possibility of faith without love and hope, no possibility of faith without social protest and healing. Such conclusions seem to lie in seminal form at the heart of the *Joint Declaration*, but the declaration's pneumatology is not sufficient to support them.

The Spirit, the Power of Faith, and the *Via Salutis*

I do not wish to emphasize what is lacking in the declaration to the extent that I do not respond to other issues which are addressed there, such as sin, the nature of our involvement in justification, and baptism. Pentecostals often preach passionate sermons against sin and the sinners. But they are also aware that we as believers must repent as well. In fact, I heard more sermons growing up that were aimed at getting the saints down to the altar to repent and be revived than evangelistic messages directed to those in the audience who may not believe. This imbalance was obviously due in part to the relative scarcity of folk present in the latter category. But I also think it was due to a conviction shared by many Pentecostals that we believers are sinners saved by grace and in constant need of revival.

On the other hand, in line with the Wesleyan/Armenian roots of Pentecostalism, the Pentecostal preaching to which I am accustomed had a very optimistic understanding of the power of active faith to lay claim to the many blessings of salvation in the here and now. In fact, the fervency and boldness involved in the expression of faith among many Pentecostals may border on blasphemy in the eyes of certain believers who may be exposed to it for the first time. Pentecostals stress the overwhelming power of God to accomplish the unexpected but focus also on the power of faith as the needed human response. Belief in the necessity of active faith is part of the Pentecostal apologetic as to why miracles are not very prevalent in the Church world today. This polemic is connected to the responsibility of believers to "do their part" by God's grace to lay claim to the many blessings of God and be a channel of these to others. "Work out your salvation with fear and trembling" was an oft-quoted text in the churches of my upbringing.

It is in the light of the above description of Pentecostal piety that I find myself in relation to the *Joint Declaration* identifying with the Lutheran emphasis on our status this side of eternity as sinners in our confrontation by the holy law of God. On the other hand, I find myself siding more with the Catholics than the Lutherans in relation to the issue of whether or not believers cooperate positively with God's grace as they are empowered by that grace to do so. One will rarely hear a sermon from a Pentecostal pulpit suggesting that we can contribute nothing to the reception or outworking of our salvation (note nos. 20–21, 29–30).

The role of baptism as the means or context through which justification is received is affirmed by both sides in the declaration as part of the biblical understanding of justification (e.g., no. 11). The role of baptism in the reception of the Spirit has been a topic of debate among Pentecostals. Many in the Oneness Pentecostal Movement (designated as such because of their modalistic understanding of the Trinity) assume that baptism is ideally and usually the context for the reception (or baptism) of the Spirit and the fulfillment of one's conversion to Christ. The Oneness Pentecostals believe that baptism in Jesus' Name provides the appropriate context for experiencing the risen Christ in the power of the Spirit in fulfillment of one's conversion. Trinitarian Pentecostals, however, tend to sharply distinguish conversion, water

baptism, and Spirit baptism (as empowerment for service; the fulfillment of one's initiation to the life of the Spirit at conversion). There is
at times a resistance among them to attribute salvific significance to
baptism. There is usually a resistance among trinitarian Pentecostals to
any hint of formalizing the reception of the Spirit in the baptismal rite.
The work of the Spirit is generally regarded as sovereign and free, and
not "bound" to a ritual of the Church.

But there are notable exceptions and variations to how trinitarian
Pentecostals talk about baptism. Walter Hollenweger tells of a typical
baptismal service in Lake Zurich, Switzerland, in which the pastor was
heard telling candidates that the water will cleanse them from every
stain and seal their commitment to follow Christ.[22] In fact, my experience in Pentecostal churches has been that water baptism is closely
linked at times to conversion/Spirit baptism in personal testimonies
and sermons. It has made me ask my Pentecostal brothers and sisters
whether or not we may not still be able to speak of "one baptism" in the
context of Pentecostal testimony, preaching, and theology. As a result, I
find myself relating with some ambivalence to the sacramental parts of
the *Joint Declaration*. The intimate link between justification and the
new-creation work of the Spirit developed above leaves open a significant role for the sacramental life of the Church. Therefore, the relationship between baptism and conversion as well as baptism and Spirit
baptism is an area that requires further reflection among Pentecostal
theologians. As I have implied throughout my discussion thus far, the
doctrine of justification will need to play a role in the context of such reflection as well, although this term has not generally played a significant role in our language of faith. It is to this fact that I turn once more.

The Doctrine by Which the Church Stands or Falls

As I have explained above, the coming kingdom of God in justice
and righteousness is an important setting for a foundationally pneumatological understanding of justification by grace through faith. Yet,
even the doctrine of the kingdom is caught up in the trinitarian faith
of the Church Catholic. In this regard, I join with others in finding it
significant that the *Joint Declaration* does not make justification the sole
criterion of theology and affirms instead a broader trinitarian faith in
paragraph 15. After all, the *regula Fidei* of the early Church was not justification explicitly but a more encompassing trinitarian confession of
God's acts of creation, self-disclosure, and redemption, as Tertullian

noted in his *The Prescriptions against the Heretics*. Here we have as the criterion of the faith the trinitarian action of God in creation by grace and a redemption by grace that includes ultimate righteousness gained by Christ and the Spirit as well as ultimate glory and healing through resurrection.

Actually, it seems doubtful that the designation of justification as *the* criterion of faith and theology can be traced to Luther. Luther did say that "the doctrine of justification must be learned diligently. For in it are included all the other doctrines of our faith; and if it is sound, all the others are sound as well."[23] But what Luther meant when he said that all other articles of faith are comprehended in this one is unclear. There is reason to believe that he regarded justification as an important source of illumination for comprehending the grounding of other truths in the grace of God revealed in Christ without denying that such truths are mutually illuminating around this center of God's gracious work in Christ. For example, Luther wrote of his discovery of justification as a gift given to faith in Romans 1:17: "My mind ran through the Scriptures as far as I was able to recollect them seeking analogies in other phrases, such as the work of God, by which he makes us strong, the wisdom of God by which he makes us wise, the strength of God, the salvation of God, the glory of God . . . "[24] In other words, justification signaled the righteousness by which God makes us righteous in Christ and this served as an analogy for how God imparts other gifts as well, such as wisdom, strength, and glory. Other truths were comprehended in justification for Luther, but not necessarily in the sense that all biblical truths are somehow deducible from justification or that justification serves a criteriological and illuminating function unattainable by other truths.

According to Risto Saarinen, the designation of justification as *the* criterion or standard (*Kriterium* or *Masstab*) of the Church and its faith which became popular in the Lutheran-Roman Catholic ecumenical discussions of the 1970s, and which has its roots in the writing of Hans Joachim Iwand and Ernst Wolf, was influenced by three factors: (1) the language of dialectical theology which viewed the Gospel as creating a "crisis" for culture, religion, and morality; (2) the critical method of Neo-Kantian philosophy which provided an analogy for theology in its use of criteria for the critique of reason; and (3) Martin Kähler's book, *Die Wissenschaft der christlichen Lehre*, which attempted to scientifically develop a dogmatic on the basis of the doctrine of justification by grace through faith. Saarinen notes that the importance of justification has at times been viewed as a material principle of foundational or central significance, or as a critical principle of hermeneutical significance in interpreting all other articles of faith aright. Though, as we have seen, the unique function of justification as *a* criterion for all other articles of faith has its roots in Luther, Saarinen implies that the exalted role of justification as *the* criterion for faith and doctrine is a relatively recent development.[25]

I have difficulty making sense of the exalted claims for justification as *the* criterion of all Christian truth, except in the sense that this confession and this doctrine point to the gracious act of redemption in Christ by the Spirit. I have recently been challenged by Eberhard Jüngel's point that justification needs to be taken seriously as *the* criterion for faith and doctrine precisely because it functions to point uniquely to the central salvific event in Christ. Jüngel criticizes Barth on this point, noting that Barth, contrary to Ernst Wolf, hesitates to grant justification an enduring role as the criterion of truth but will then inconsistently refer to justification as pointing uniquely to the gracious act of redemption in Christ.[26]

But if justification points uniquely to the Christ event, so do other metaphors of salvation by the Spirit in Christ. Justification and sanctification are overlapping metaphors for God's act of redemption in Christ. One could view terms like justification and sanctification as metaphors of redemption through Christ in the Spirit, each from a different vantage point and context. What I have done with justification in the context of the just fulfillment of God's covenant promises to creation, could be done with sanctification from the vantage point of the cult and its implications for the sanctification of creation.

In summary, I affirm the significant accomplishment of the *Joint Declaration* in clarifying the issues that divided the Western Church of the sixteenth century and in seeking common agreements across the divides of enduring disagreements. Such an effort was needed as a foundation for further discussion of the issue. But we would do the declaration a terrible injustice if we were to think that the matter of justification is now settled, so that we can proceed on to other matters, or that all that is left to do is to draw out the ecclesiological or ethical implications of the declaration. I view the declaration as a fine negotiation of sixteenth-century tensions in the light of certain points drawn from twentieth-century biblical research and ecumenical discussions. But much more work is needed on an ecumenical understanding of justification that is not so bound to sixteenth-century presuppositions and tensions as this current declaration is. I trust that this interaction with the *Joint Declaration* can represent some stimulation toward that important end.

Notes

[1] Miroslav Volf, "Materiality of Salvation: An Investigation in the Soteriologies of Liberation and Pentecostal Theologies," *Journal of Ecumenical Studies* (Summer 1989) 447–67.

[2] Walter J. Hollenweger, *The Pentecostals* (Peabody, Mass.: Hendrickson, 1972, 1988) 316–17.

[3] Gustaf Aulén, *Christus Victor: A Historical Study of the Three Main Types of the Idea of the Atonement* (New York: Macmillan, 1969).

[4] Carl E. Braaten and Robert W. Jenson, eds., *Union with Christ: The New Finnish Interpretation of Luther* (Grand Rapids, Mich.: Eerdmans, 1998). See also Veli-Matti Karkkainen, "Deification and a Pneumatological Concept of Grace: Unprecedented Convergences between Eastern Orthodox, Lutheran, and Pentecostal-Holiness Soteriologies." Paper presented at the annual meeting of the Society for Pentecostal Studies, Springfield, Missouri, March 1998.

[5] Geoffrey Wainwright, "Rechtfertigung: lutherisch oder katholisch?" *Kerygma und Dogma* 45, 182–206.

[6] Hans Küng, *Justification: The Doctrine of Karl Barth and a Catholic Reflection* (Philadelphia: Westminster, 1981) 213ff.

[7] Ibid.

[8] Harding Meyer, "The Text 'The Justification of the Sinner' in the Context of Previous Ecumenical Dialogues on Justification," in Karl Lehmann, Michael Root, and William G. Rusch, eds., *Justification by Faith: Do the Sixteenth-Century Condemnations Still Apply?* (New York: Continuum, 1999) 82.

[9] Note, for example, Jürgen Moltmann, *The Spirit of Life: A Universal Affirmation* (Minneapolis: Fortress, 1992); Clark Pinnock, *Flame of Love: A Theology of the Holy Spirit* (Downers Grove, Ill.: Intervarsity, 1996); James Dunn, *Jesus and the Spirit: A Study of the Religious and Charismatic Experience of Jesus and the First Christians Reflected in the New Testament* (Grand Rapids: Eerdmans, 1997).

[10] Frank Macchia, *Spirituality and Social Liberation: The Message of the Blumhardts in the Light of Wuerttemberg Pietism* (Metuchen, N.J.: Scarecrow Press, 1993).

[11] Christoph Blumhardt, *Ansprache, Predigten, Reden, Briefe: 1865–1917*, V. 2 (Neukirchen, Germany: Neukirchener Verlag, 1978) 5.

[12] Jürgen Moltmann, "Was heisst heute 'evangelisch'? Von der Rechtfertigungslehre zur Reich-Gottes-Theologie," *Evangelische Theologie* 57 (1997) 41–46.

[13] Brevard Childs, *Biblical Theology of the Old and New Testaments: Theological Reflection on the Christian Bible* (Minneapolis: Fortress, 1992) 488–99.

[14] Hans Heinrich Schmid, "Rechtfertigung als Schöpfungsgeschehen: Notizen zur alttestamentlichen Vorgeschichte eines neutestamentlichen Themas," Johannes Friedrich, Wolfgang Polmann, and Peter Stuhlmacher, eds., *Rechtfertigung: Festschrift für Ernst Käsemann zum 70 Geburtstag* (Tübingen: J.C.B. Mohr, 1976) 406.

[15] Thomas Finger, "An Anabaptist Perspective on Justification," in Milan Opocensky and Raemonn Paraic, eds., *Justification and Sanctification in the Traditions of the Reformation: Prague V, the Fifth Consultation on the First and Second Reformations, Geneva, 13 to 17*

February 1998, Studies from the World Alliance of Reformed Churches, no. 42 (Geneva: World Alliance of Reformed Churches, 1999) 57.

[16] Ernst Käsemann, "The Righteousness of God in Paul,"in *New Testament Questions of Today* (Philadelphia: Fortress Press, 1969) 168–82.

[17] I am grateful to Lyle Dabney for originally drawing my attention to the significance of Romans 4:25 and the resurrection of Christ for justification: "Justified in the Spirit: Soteriological Reflections on the Resurrection," paper presented at the annual meeting of the American Academy of Religion, Orlando, 1998.

[18] Joseph Fitzmeyer, *Romans*, The Anchor Bible (New York: Doubleday, 1992) 389.

[19] Charles Hodge, *Epistle to the Romans*, 9th ed. (Grand Rapids, Mich.: Eerdmans, 1958) 129.

[20] Everett F. Harrison, *Romans*, vol. 10, The Expositor's Bible Commentary (Grand Rapids, Mich.: Zondervan, 1976) 54.

[21] Jürgen Moltmann, "Was heisst heute 'evangelisch'?" 44–45.

[22] Walter Hollenweger, *The Pentecostals*, 390–95.

[23] Martin Luther, *Lectures on Galatians* (1535) in Jaroslav Pelikan, ed., *Luther's Works*, vol. 26 (St. Louis: Concordia Publishing House, 1963) 283.

[24] Translation taken from H. J. Hillenbrand, ed., *The Reformation: A Narrative History Related by Contemporary Observers and Participants* (Grand Rapids, Mich.: Baker Book House, 1978) 27–28.

[25] Risto Saarinen, "Die Rechtfertigung als Kriterium," *Kirche und Dogma* 44, 88–103.

[26] Eberhard Jüngel, *Das Evangelium von der Rechtfertigung des Gottlösen als Zentrum des christlichen Glaubens: Eine Theologische Studie in ökumenischer Absicht*, 2nd ed. (Mohr Siebeck, 1999) esp. 15–26.